Paris

Renée Grimaud

PARIS

Translated by
NATALIE DANFORD

METRO BOOKS
NEW YORK

Paris

Opposite: The Eiffel Tower is the most recognizable landmark in Paris.

P. 2: The large clock in the old Orsay railway station, today the main entry hall to the Musée d'Orsay, dedicated to late 19th-century art.

Paris

Opposite: Notre-Dame is the most popular tourist attraction in Paris, and also one of its oldest—the cathedral's first brick was laid in 1163. It rises like a beacon on the Île de la Cité and can be seen from afar. The Seine runs below it; the river's famed *bateaux-mouches* now serve mainly tourists.
Pp. 8-9: The Opéra Garnier, designed by Charles Garnier during the Second Empire, is decorated with busts of composers. Its eclectic decor is typical of the Napoleon III era. Note the N and E on the medallions— the initials of the emperor and his wife. Opera and ballet are performed here.

Paris

Opposite: The Fontaine de l'Observatoire, also known as the fountain of the four parts of the world, sits in the gardens of the Paris Observatory on the wide, shady avenue named for it. This elegant monument was built by Gabriel Davioud in the 19th century. The bronze statue of the four parts of the world (Africa, America, Asia, and Europe) is by Jean-Baptiste Carpeaux; the seahorses are by Emmanuel Frémiet.

Pp. 12-13: There are only two original subway signs —those designed by Art Nouveau master Hector Guimard in the late 19th century—left in the capital: the one for the Abbesses stop in the 18th Arrondissement (shown here) and the one for Porte-Dauphine. The iron and glass signs are graced with curved lines and floral motifs, both signatures of Guimard.

Pp. 14-15: The chimeras were added to Notre-Dame in 1850 by architect Eugène Viollet-le-Duc during restoration. Although they were not originally part of the building, they have become one of its most famous features. A close-up view can be seen from the top of the cathedral's towers.

Pp. 16-17: The first public clock in Paris dates to 1370 and is in the clock tower of the Palais de la Cité, residence of the kings in the Middle Ages.

METRO BOOKS
New York

An Imprint of Sterling Publishing Co., Inc.
1166 Avenue of the Americas
New York, NY 10036

© 2018 METRO BOOKS and the distinctive Metro Books logo are registered trademarks of Sterling Publishing Co., Inc.

First edition © 2015 Sassi Editore Srl

All rights reserved. No part of this publication may be reproduced, stored in a retrieval system, or transmitted in any form or by any means (including electronic, mechanical, photocopying, recording, or otherwise) without prior written permission from the publisher.

ISBN 978-1-4351-6787-2

For information about custom editions, special sales, and premium and corporate purchases, please contact Sterling Special Sales at 800-805-5489 or specialsales@sterlingpublishing.com.

Manufactured in China

2 4 6 8 10 9 7 5 3 1

www.sterlingpublishing.com

© Texts, Renée Grimaud
Translator: Natalie Danford
© Images, as in the photographic credits

SACRA DEI
CELEBRARE PIVS
REGALE TIME
IVS

Contents

Introduction	25
The Heart of the City of Light	31
Île de la Cité – Louvre – Palais-Royal – Hôtel de Ville – Marais – Temple	
From the Latin Quarter to the Seine	79
Panthéon – Luxembourg – Saint-Germain des Prés – Palais-Bourbon Invalides – Eiffel Tower	
From Opéra-Bastille to the Villette	121
Popincourt – Reuilly – Ménilmontant – Belleville République – Buttes-Chaumont	
From the Champs-Elysées to Montmartre	145
Élysée – Opéra – Grands Boulevards – Butte Montmartre Batignolles-Monceau – Bois de Boulogne	
The Royal Residences	197
Versailles – Fontainebleau – Vaux-le-Vicomte – Chantilly	
Photographic credits	240

Paris

Pp. 18-19: The unique colored tubes on the exterior of the Centre Georges Pompidou, home to the modern art museum. Since opening in 1977, the building has been the subject of heated debate, but early criticism has turned to admiration, and today the center is considered an excellent example of contemporary architecture.
Pp. 20-21: Another symbol of contemporary architecture in Paris is the pyramid at the Louvre, by I.M. Pei, erected in 1989 to mark the bicentennial of the French Revolution. This, too, was harshly criticized at first, but today it has become an admired part of the Louvre complex. The proportions are the same as those of the Egyptian pyramid in Giza.
Opposite: Pont Alexandre III is one of the most beautiful bridges in Paris. It was built for the World's Fair of 1900. In the distance is the Montparnasse Tower, which rises more than 200 meters (656 feet) in the air over the city. The bridge leads to Les Invalides on the Left Bank, recognizable by its gold leaf-covered dome.

Paris

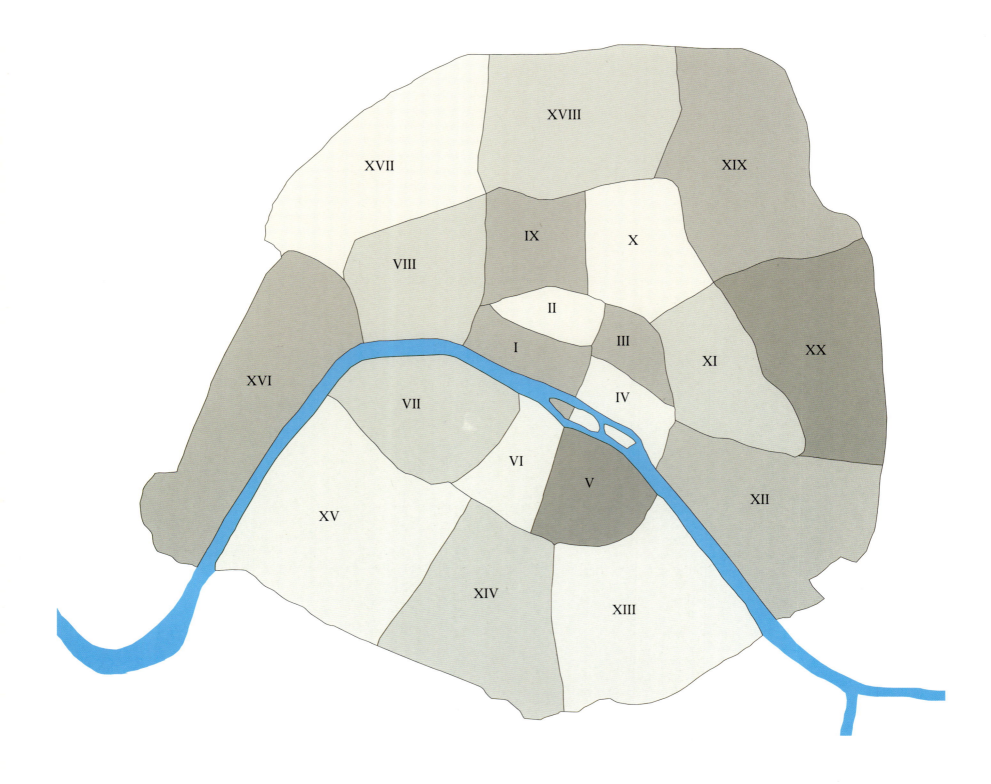

Arrondissements

I - Louvre

II - Bourse

III - Temple

IV - Hôtel-de-Ville

V - Panthéon

VI - Luxembourg

VII - Palais-Bourbon

VIII - Élysée

IX - Opéra

X - Enclos-Saint-Laurent

XI - Popincourt

XII - Reuilly

XIII - Gobelins

XIV - Observatoire

XV - Vaugirard

XVI - Passy

XVII - Batignolles-Monceau

XVIII - Butte-Montmartre

XIX - Buttes-Chaumont

XX - Ménilmontant

INTRODUCTION

Pp. 26-27: The Eiffel Tower is the most famous emblem of Paris. Built by engineer Gustave Eiffel for the 1889 World's Fair, this metal masterpiece stands 300 meters (982 feet) tall. Visitors need to walk 1,652 steps to reach the top—or they can take the elevator. The tower is seen here from the gardens at Trocadéro; in the foreground is the lovely *Flora* statue by Louis Lejeune.

Paris is often described as the world's most beautiful city, and while there's no absolute measure of such things, it is certainly one of the world's most fascinating and unforgettable cities. No matter how many times you visit Paris, it will reveal something new to you upon arrival. The Seine winds through Paris and has shaped it in numerous ways. Rive droite, rive gauche: The French capital is a place of constant dualism. The Seine divides the city, but its banks are connected by fantastic structures such as the Pont Neuf and the Pont Alexandre III, so it is also a unifying force.

Indeed, the banks of the Seine are such a precious place, much appreciated for the opportunity they present to stroll at length, that they are listed on the UNESCO World Heritage list. Each year, the banks of the Seine are the site of Paris-Plages, and in all seasons the Seine is home to a number of lucky houseboat residents. The sunrise and sunset over the Seine may be the most spectacular sight in Paris.

The city has no shortage of breathtaking views, including the view from the towering heights of the Eiffel Tower, the Arc de Triomphe, and the Montparnasse Tower. But underground Paris—with its catacombs, sewers, and water system—is intriguing as well. The city might be approached via its parks and gardens, or following a chronological itinerary, since history seems to come alive here on every block. For lovers of the arts, of course, Paris offers a wealth of museums of every variety. But perhaps the best way to understand the soul of this city is to sit outside at a café and observe passersby, or just to walk its streets, eyes open to the possibilities, and enjoy all the unexpected architectural details. The Petite Ceinture, a former railway, is a fascinating place, as are the romantically unkempt cemeteries of Paris. And there are still neighborhoods where unknown artists toil away behind walls and doors. Though more and more such courtyards and alleyways are closed off from view, Paris is still a city that offers numerous chances to stumble across the unexpected and to enjoy a spontaneous discovery.

At night, Paris is even more magical. Light hits the soaring arches of churches as they draw elegant arabesques through the sky, and it reflects off the river to create eye-catching streaks. The Eiffel Tower sparkles with light, while the profile of the glass and steel pyramid at the Louvre is thrown into stark relief.

Lutetia, the Roman city that would become Paris, was born on the Île de la Cité in the middle of the Seine. It then expanded to the Left Bank, on the slopes of the Latin Quarter. The river was a true commercial artery in those days, and the powerful boatmen's association that formed was responsible for transporting goods.

Later, the Franks took over the city and gave it the name it still bears today. Their ruler, King Clovis, made it the capital of his kingdom. In the Middle Ages the Sorbonne university, founded in the 13th century, attracted students and scholars from all over Europe. Paris became a cultural center and also one of the centers of Gothic art and architecture. Masterpieces of the style, such as Notre-Dame and Sainte Chapelle, would make the City of Light one of the beacons of Christianity.

Under the Valois and the Bourbons, the city expanded and grew more ornate. The royal palace of the Louvre reached its current size. Louis XIV, the Sun King, surrounded himself with glamour in the places he ordered built to celebrate his power, such as Les Invalides. The heart of the Enlightenment under Louis XV, Paris saw one of its mythical buildings, the Bastille, fall victim to the axes brandished by revolutionaries during the French Revolution.

Napoleon brought the city back from a dark place with arches and columns celebrating his military victories, and then five years later Georges-Eugène Haussmann arrived and undertook major works, commissioned by

Napoleon III, that radically transformed the city, which until then had remained largely Medieval in character. The broad new boulevards and impressive stone buildings would redefine the Paris of the Second Empire. From the late 19th century to the time of World War II, Paris attracted artists in all fields who expressed their talent to its fullest, making it a barometer for trends in the art world. Today there are numerous avant-garde buildings around the city's periphery. The Zoo de Vincennes has been renovated from top to bottom. In the Tolbiac neighborhood in the 13th Arrondissement stands the Très Grande Bibliothèque; the Joséphine Baker floating pool makes it possible to swim on the Seine every summer. The Cité de la Mode e du Design looks like a bright lime-green lizard posing lazily. The Simone de Beauvoir biking and walking path is an undulating ribbon that leads to the Parc de Bercy in the 12th Arrondissement. The Grands Moulins of

ABOVE: AT NIGHT THE PYRAMID AT THE LOUVRE IS EVEN MORE STRIKING. ITS GLASS WALLS ARE REFLECTED IN THE WATER AROUND IT.

Paris have been transformed into university buildings. In the west, in the Bois de Boulogne, the Louis Vuitton Foundation building was constructed in 2014 based on a Frank Gehry design.

Tourists are a constant in Paris, and they arrive from all over the world. In the 17th century, they marveled at the world's first public lighting system and went home to astonish others with their descriptions of a city that never fell into darkness. At the time, Nicolas de la Reynie, the first lieutenant general of police appointed by Jean-Baptiste Colbert, had streetlights installed to discourage thieves from committing crimes. From that less-than-romantic motive, Paris earned the extremely romantic moniker the City of Light, and it still bears that name today, as it basks in the reflected glow of its past and also looks toward a promising future.

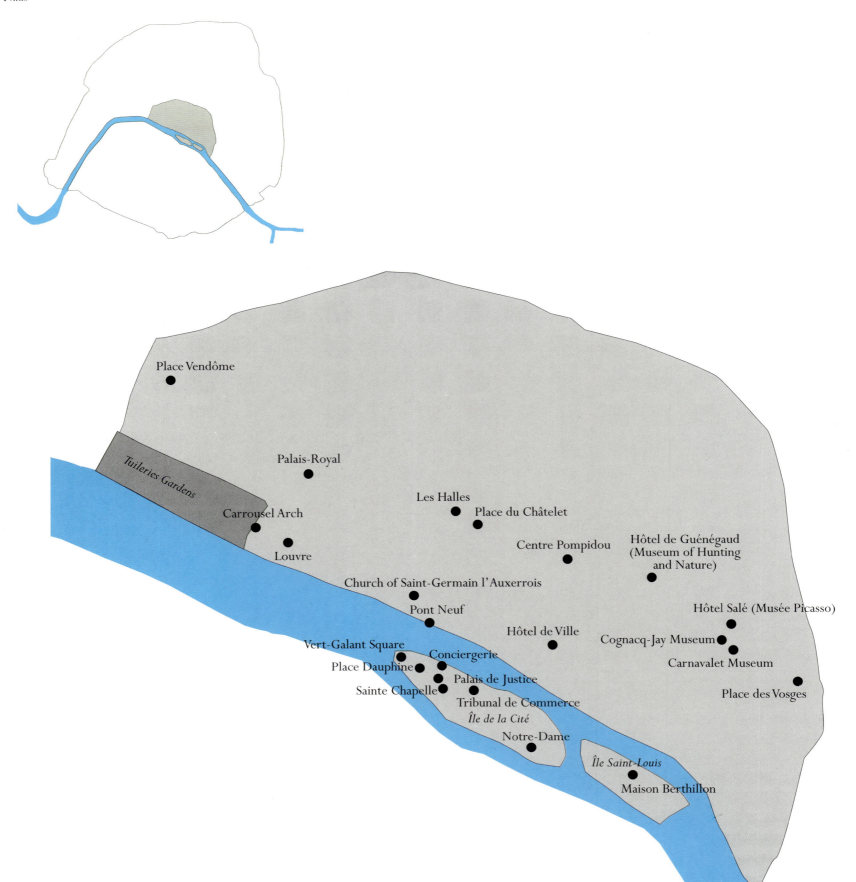

The Heart of the City of Light

Île de la Cité — Louvre — Palais-Royal — Hôtel de Ville
Marais — Temple

Ancient Paris developed along the banks of the Seine. Lutetia, the Roman city, was founded on the Île de la Cité and from there expanded toward the higher ground of the Latin Quarter. The roots of France's capital can still be seen in the parvis of Notre-Dame with its archeological crypt (where the floodgates from the Gallo-Roman era can be viewed) and in the overall look of the stunning cathedral, a Gothic masterpiece whose tall towers stretch toward the heavens. It took almost two centuries to build this marvel of balance and structure, and it is one of the most recognizable sights in Paris. The cathedral was the stage for crucial episodes in French history: Henry, King of Navarre, who would go on to become Henry IV, married Marguerite de Valois there (though as a Protestant he had to remain outside in the parvis!) and Napoleon had himself crowned emperor there. During the French Revolution the cathedral's statues were damaged, its bells were melted down, and it was transformed into the Temple of Reason.

Not far away, in the heart of the ancient royal palace—today the main courthouse—Sainte-Chapelle attracted attention with its immense windows, which allowed in rays of light so intense that the faithful in the Middle Ages called the building a "door to heaven." The chapel was built by Louis IX to house the relics of the Passion of Christ. From here, visitors can walk to the western edge of Île de la Cité, where they arrive at Vert-Galant. The name was a nickname for Henry IV, a statue of whom stands on the Pont-Neuf. The king ordered the construction of this neighborhood around the Place Dauphine, with its lovely rows of tall stone and brick houses alternating with swank restaurants.

From Île de la Cité, the Pont Saint-Louis leads to Île Saint-Louis, a peaceful and cozy spot that has preserved its sumptuous private homes from the 17th century where the elite lived at the time of Louis XIV. Parisians come to picnic on the tranquil banks of the Île Saint-Louis on Sundays. The spirit of writers such as Charles Baudelaire, Théophile Gautier, and Louis Aragon can still be felt in the area, where they and other writers lived and wrote many of their essential works. This street is also home to a very famous ice cream shop, the Maison Berthillon, where locals and tourists alike line up impatiently to taste the refined and delicious flavors available inside.

The kings left their mark on the Louvre, which was a royal residence before it became one of the largest museums in the world. The history of this extraordinary museum begins in the 12th century, when Phillip II built a fortress to protect Paris from English invasions. Two centuries later, Charles V modernized and expanded the Louvre, creating a library for his incredible manuscript collection—the origins of the national library. The foundations of his castle are still visible today. In the 1500s, Francis I knocked down the tall tower and in its place built a Renaissance palace that his successors would continue to improve upon over the centuries. In 1989, Chinese architect I.M. Pei made his contribution with his famous pyramid, fit to compete with the collections inside, which include classics such as the *Nike of Samothrace*, the *Venus de Milo*, and, of course, the one painting no visitor wants to miss, the extremely famous *Mona Lisa*. The renovation under the Grand Louvre plan has gone hand-in-hand with beautification of the

Pp. 32-33: The Napoleon Courtyard at the Louvre displays a seamless combination of the ancient and the modern. The elegant Pavillon de Marsan, which contains the decorative arts collection, was rebuilt under Napoleon III. In the center of the courtyard is I.M. Pei's famous pyramid, surrounded by smaller pyramids and triangular reflecting pools. On the far side are the Carrousel arch, which marks the entrance to the Tuileries gardens, and a large Ferris wheel.

Pp. 34-35: The Napoleon Courtyard at the Louvre contains more than eighty statues of famous figures.
Opposite: This equestrian statue in the Napoleon Courtyard at the Louvre depicts a young Louis XIV. I.M. Pei, the architect responsible for the pyramid, placed it here to mark the axis of the Champs-Élysées. The statue was made of lead using Bernini's original marble version as a mold.
Pp. 38-39: At night the larger and smaller pyramids at the Louvre are lit up and transform the ancient building into something otherworldly.

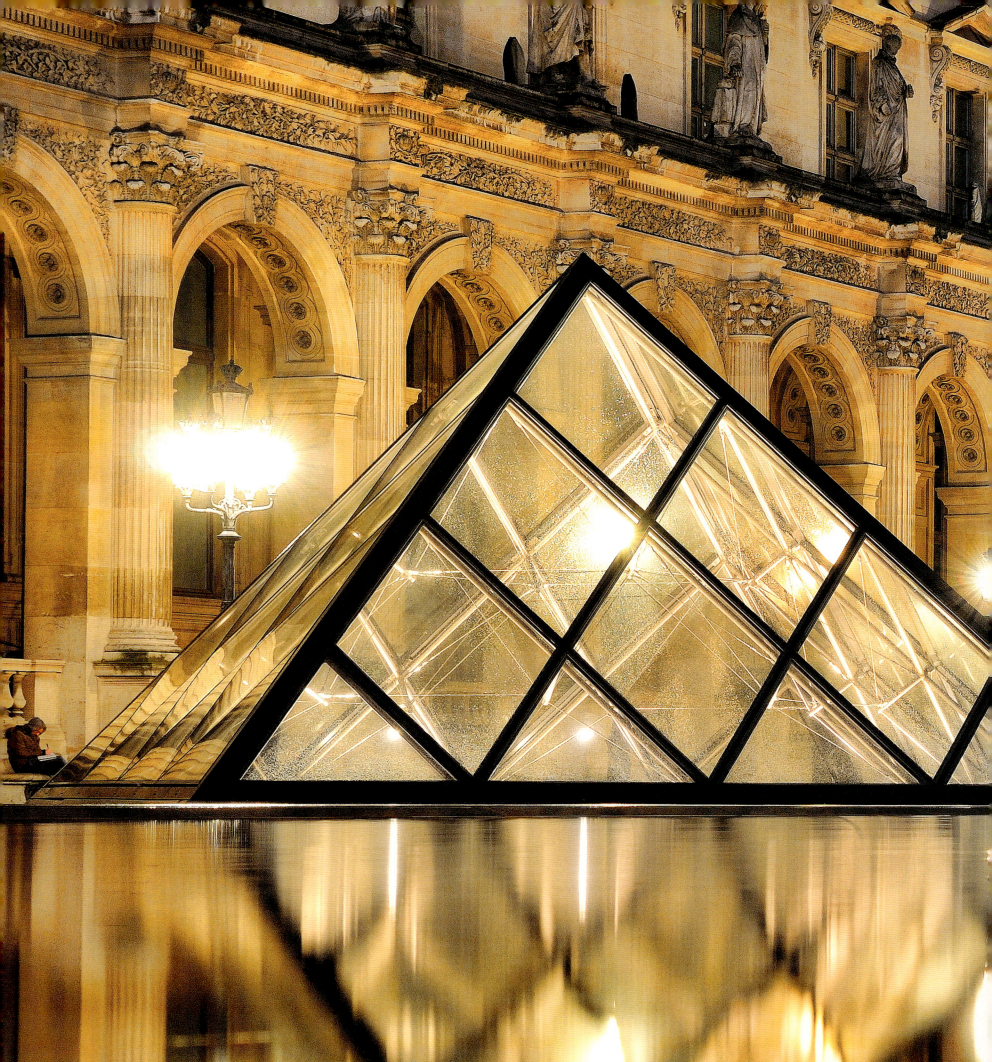

Pp. 40-41: The Pavillon de Mollien at the Louvre, seen from the side of the Napoleon Courtyard, is decorated with caryatids by François Jouffroy dating to 1857 and plenty of flowers and fruit.
Opposite: The apartments of Anne of Austria, the mother of Louis XIV, were sumptuously decorated by architect Louis Le Vau. Today they house collections of Roman antiquities. The rooms are decorated with stuccos credited largely to sculptor Michel Anguier; Athena, identified by her helmet, wears armor with a relief depicting Louis XIV.

The Heart of the City of Light

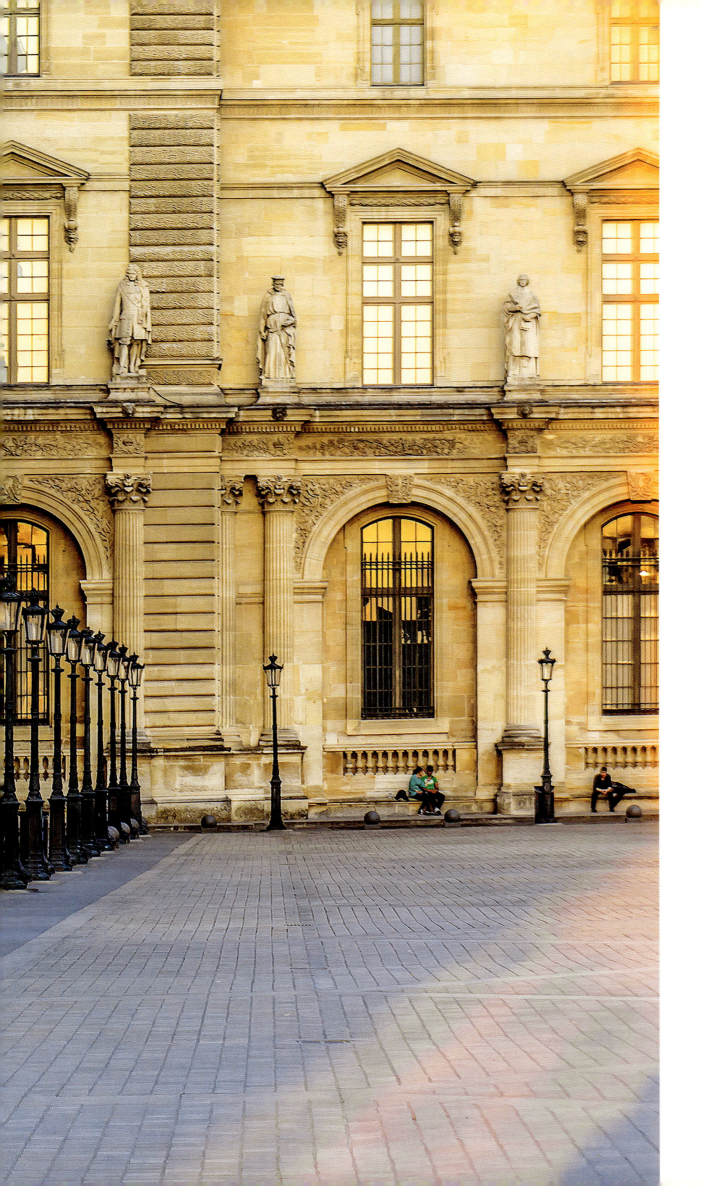

Opposite: The Louvre includes the Grande Galérie, which dates to the era of Henry IV, and on the Rue de Rivoli side a series of buildings constructed under Napoleon and Napoleon III.
P. 46: Close-up of the gorgeous main gate at the western entrance to the Tuileries gardens from the Place de la Concorde.
P. 47: *Renommée* riding Pegasus by Antoine Coysevox, sculptor in the era of Louis XIV. This statue on the gate to the Tuileries is a concrete copy (the original is in the Marly Courtyard at the Louvre).
Pp. 48-49: The Pavillon de Marsan and the north wing of the Louvre hold the museum's decorative arts collection, one of the best in the world. Exhibition spaces in these parts of the building have been thoughtfully renovated in recent years.

OPPOSITE: IN THE TUILERIES, ON THE TERRASSE DU BORD DE L'EAU IN FRONT OF THE FLORA PAVILION, STANDS A GROUP OF SCULPTURES BY PAUL LANDOWSKI KNOWN AS *THE SONS OF CAIN*. TO THE LEFT IS THE SHEPHERD, JABEL; IN THE CENTER IS THE POET, JUBAL; AND TO THE RIGHT IS THE BLACKSMITH, TUBAL-CAIN, KEEPER OF THE FLAME. LANDOWSKI BASED THE FIGURES ON THREE YOUNG TUNISIANS HE MET WHILE TRAVELING.

ABOVE: NAPOLEON HIRED ARCHITECTS CHARLES PERCIER AND PIERRE FONTAINE TO DESIGN THE TRIUMPHAL ENTRANCE TO THE TUILERIES PALACE. IT HAD BEEN DESTROYED DURING THE DAYS OF THE COMMUNE, AND THE CARROUSEL TRIUMPHAL ARCH HAD REMAINED ISOLATED; TODAY IT SERVES AS THE ENTRANCE TO THE TUILERIES GARDENS. INSPIRED BY ROMAN ARCHES, IT IS FLANKED BY EIGHT WHITE AND PINK MARBLE COLUMNS. THE RELIEFS DEPICT IMPERIAL VICTORIES IN 1805. AT THE TOP IS A GODDESS ACCOMPANIED BY THE VICTORIES, WHO LEAD HORSES, SYMBOL OF THE RESTORATION. THIS GROUP OF SCULPTURES REPLACED THE HORSES FROM SAINT MARK'S BASILICA, WHICH WERE RETURNED TO VENICE IN 1815.

Tuileries gardens and the Place du Carrousel. As a result, the forty hectares (ninety-nine acres) between the Seine and the Rue de Rivoli have become one of the loveliest parts of Paris.

The less well-known Palais-Royal was called the Palais-Cardinal in the time of Cardinal Richelieu, as it belonged to that very powerful minister under Louis XIII. Just before he died, Richelieu decided to offer his palace to the king—that was when it came to be known as the Palais-Royal. Today it is home to three institutions: the Ministry of Culture, the Council of State, and the Constitutional Council. These days, while strolling through the gardens, which are surrounded by *galeries* lined with boutiques, it's almost inconceivable that during the French Revolution this was a focal point of Parisian unrest, or that during the time of the Consulate and then the Empire, it was in the hands of thieves, gamblers, and prostitutes.

Near the Palais-Royal, Rue Saint-Honoré leads to Les Halles. This giant market, which Émile Zola once deemed the "belly of Paris" because it was the major source of food for the entire city since the Middle Ages, was replaced in the 1960s by a large retail shopping center, despite vigorous protest from Parisians. The area is also an important railway hub where the city's subway and the local commuter train lines cross. Les Halles is currently being renovated: the upper part will be covered by the Canopée, an undulating canopy structure that takes its inspiration from plants and which will completely change the look of the entire neighborhood. All around Les Halles, the gardens are to be rejuvenated as well.

On the other side of the Boulevard Sébastopol, a wide artery that is often jammed with traffic and that is lined with wholesale stores, stands the Centre Georges Pompidou, designed by Italian architect Renzo Piano and opened in 1977. It was the subject of heated debate at the time. The building, with its series of colored tubes visible on the outside, has been compared to an oil refinery, a factory, and a shipyard, though the architect said his aim was to "put the inside on the outside and display the inner workings." The center was named for the French president who undertook the project and is the largest modern art museum in Europe. This multidisciplinary

Pp. 52-53: The triumphal arch of Carrousel. Close-up of the quadriga, the Victories, and the horses. The statues depicting Napoleon's soldiers have suffered from pollution and are in poor condition.

Above: In the center of the Place Vendôme where the Rue de la Paix crosses the Rue de Castiglione, a column was erected to honor Napoleon's imperial forces. The column is modeled on Trajan's Column in Rome. This historic square was designed by Jules Hardouin-Mansart, architect under Louis XIV. There are 176 steps to the top of the column, where Napoleon is depicted in the guise of a Roman emperor, holding a sword and a globe topped with a winged Victory.

Opposite: Close-up of the Vendôme column, whose decorations depict the victory at Austerlitz in 1805. To create this monument, 1,200 cannons were taken from the Austrians and melted down to obtain 150 tons of bronze.

P. 56 and p. 57: The church of Saint-Germain l'Auxerrois, in front of the Louvre arcade, has a flamboyantly Gothic portico. After suffering great damage, it was restored in the 19th century when the square was transformed by Baron Haussmann. The statues of the founding saints date to that time. On August 24, 1572, the bells of Saint-Germain l'Auxerrois rang to mark the Saint Bartholomew's Day massacre, a tragic episode in the French Wars of Religion.

P. 58-59: The Tribunal de Commerce building with its dome was built under Napoleon III. The adjacent small Place Louis Lépine hosts a daily flower market. Boats of all kinds float along the Seine. The Conciergerie on the Quai de l'Horloge was part of a royal palace in the Middle Ages. It then became a prison and Marie Antoinette was held there during the French Revolution before she met her fate at the guillotine. The building's clock tower with its rectangular base dates to the 14th century and was the first public clock in Paris.

OPPOSITE: LIGHTS ON THE PONT NEUF AND THE STATUE OF HENRY IV, A REPLICA OF THE ORIGINAL. THE SCULPTOR PLACED VARIOUS DOCUMENTS AND OBJECTS IN THE BASE OF THE PEDESTAL, INCLUDING BOOKS ON HENRY IV, COINS, AND MEDALS.
PP. 62-63: THE TOWERS AND THE APSE OF NOTRE-DAME WITH THE SPIRE THAT WAS ADDED BY EUGÈNE VIOLLET-LE-DUC IN THE 19TH CENTURY. THE ARCHITECT IMPLEMENTED RESTORATION BECAUSE THE CATHEDRAL WAS SERIOUSLY DAMAGED DURING THE FRENCH REVOLUTION. ALL AROUND, AN ELEGANT SQUARE PROVIDES ROOM FOR RELAXING AND WATCHING THE BOATS CRUISING THE SEINE. THE SMALL PONT AU DOUBLE LEADS TO THE LATIN QUARTER.
PP. 64-65: THE LARGE ROSE WINDOW OF THE CATHEDRAL IS AN AMAZING TEN METERS (THIRTY-THREE FEET) IN DIAMETER. ITS DESIGN WAS CONSIDERED SO PERFECT THAT IT WAS UNTOUCHED AFTER ITS INITIAL CREATION. AT THE BASE IS THE VIRGIN WITH CHILD, SURROUNDED BY ANGELS.
PP. 66-67: THE CATHEDRAL'S NAVE IS LIKE A STONE VESSEL SUPPORTED BY POWERFUL VAULTS AND ILLUMINATED BY ENORMOUS WINDOWS. ITS HEIGHT IS A TESTAMENT TO THE TALENT OF 13TH-CENTURY ARCHITECTS AND ALLOWS THE INTERIOR TO BE BRIGHTLY LIT.

cultural space holds exhibitions, conferences, shows, concerts—it's a public library as much as a museum. On a clear day, visitors riding its external escalators can see all the way to the white domes of the Sacré-Coeur Basilica in Montmartre.

Moving toward the Seine, the next stop is the Place du Châtelet, surrounded by two twin theaters built as part of the construction commissioned by Baron Georges-Eugène Haussmann, who transformed Paris during the second half of the 19th century. Here in the Middle Ages the Grand Châtelet was built as a fortress to protect the Île de la Cité. In the center of the square stands the Fontaine du Palmier, which dates to the Napoleonic era and is surrounded by gilded bronze rings to commemorate the emperor's victories; the same symbol can be spotted in other places around Paris. You've got to be in good shape to walk up the 300 steps of the Saint-Jacques Tower that was once a destination for pilgrims along the Santiago de Compostela route. The fantastic panoramic view of Paris from the top is its own reward. Moving eastward leads to the square in front of the Hôtel de Ville with its contemporary fountains. In winter an outdoor skating rink fills the square, and in summer it is the site of soccer games, especially during the Paris-Plages, held every year on the banks of the Seine. It was Étienne Marcel, provost of the merchants and a member of the Parisian bourgeoisie, who floated the idea for the earliest form of municipality (limiting the king's power) in 1357. The Seine greatly influenced the development of business in Paris, as the river could be used to transport almost anything the capital needed (and the boatmen once formed a very powerful group). During the Renaissance, the Hôtel de Ville was transformed into a luxurious palace in accordance with the designs of Italian architect Domenico da Cortona, also known as Boccador. Destroyed in 1871 during the Paris Commune era, it was later rebuilt in identical form and it is still the seat of city government today. There is no sign, however, of the fact that for five centuries this large, sloping square redesigned by Haussmann witnessed many state-sponsored executions. In those days, it was known as the Place de Grève. One of the many people killed here was François Ravaillac, who assassinated Henry IV.

The Rue des Archives, a lively street lined with stores and cafés, leads to the Marais. This picturesque Parisian neighborhood—probably the city's most pleasant and most crowded with private homes and museums—was actually almost knocked down in the 1960s. It was saved at the last minute by André Malraux, who was minister for cultural affairs at the time. This is a popular spot with tourists, who flock to the area's contemporary galleries and fashionable boutiques, many of which are housed in former bakeries whose historic facades have been preserved. This is also the main neighborhood in Paris for gay culture. This area was once swampland that was often flooded (hence the name Marais, which means swamp). It was first occupied in the Middle Ages by several different religious orders, including those of the Order of the Temple. There was grazing land and fertile farmland here as well, and grains and legumes were once cultivated.

Beginning in the 15th century, the kings of France invested heavily in this part of the capital. Charles V and Henry II had many buildings constructed here, though they are now gone. Aristocrats followed in their wake: Over the course of two centuries, the Marais was transformed. New buildings such as the

Paris

Opposite: Notre-Dame's apse and its fifteen-meter (forty-nine-foot) buttresses make the building stable. The spire destroyed during the French Revolution was rebuilt by Eugène Viollet-le-Duc; it rises ninety meters (295 feet) in the air. In the center of the Square Jean XXIII there is a fountain dedicated to the Virgin Mary. The church faces the square.

home of the Lamoignon family and that of the Sully family sprung up. The creation of the Place des Vosges in the early 17th century—built at the behest of Henry IV—completed the evolution. Ministers, magistrates, bankers, aristocrats, and other members of the elite were followed by literati and artists. Everyone, it seemed, wanted his own building in the Marais. After the French Revolution, aristocrats expatriated and the buildings were abandoned bit by bit until the neighborhood was populated by craftspeople and merchants and changed its look yet again. In the 19th century, Jewish refugees from Central Europe gave the Marais yet another new identity as they settled around the Rue des Rosiers, the Rue des Écouffes, and the Rue Ferdinand Duval. Many places recount this history, including the synagogue on Rue Pavée (decorated by Hector Guimard), the one on Rue des Tournelles (credited to Gustave Eiffel), the Museum of Jewish Art and History, and the Memorial of the Deportation (where the names of thousands of French Jews deported during World War II are engraved). Beautifully restored, the old private homes of the Marais are for the most part museums today. The Hôtel Salé is famous for its staircase formed by two ramps and ending with a balcony, and it is home to the Musée

Above: As intended by the architect, the Centre Georges Pompidou's structure is completely visible; its elevators and escalators are transparent. Each color has a meaning: the red elements are for circulation. Street musicians often play in the square in front of the building, where the workshop of Romanian sculptor Constantin Brancusi has been recreated.

Pp. 72-73: The painted tubes of the Centre Georges Pompidou once prompted critics to compare the building to an oil refinery. Their color indicates their function: blue pipes are for air conditioning and heating, while the green pipes are for plumbing.

Picasso and its impressive collections. The Hôtel de Guénégaud is now the Museum of Hunting and Nature, overhauled and updated with original contributions from contemporary artists. The Cognacq-Jay Museum, which takes its name from the owner of the Samaritaine, one of the largest Parisian department stores until the 19th century, concentrates on 18th-century art. The city's own history is the subject under the magnifying glass at the Carnavalet Museum. This 17th-century jewel holds a varied and eclectic collection that ranges from the Neolithic canoes (more than 6,000 years old) excavated in the Bercy area to the Hôtel de Wendel ballroom from the early 1900s. Models of monuments, signs, paintings, and objects from the period of the French Revolution are just some of the more than 600,000 items collected in this extraordinary museum, which really does feel like a portal to a Paris of an earlier time. North of the Marais, in the area known as Haut Marais, there are stores selling organic items, beauty products, and other high-concept retail outlets all around the Rue de Bretagne that attract a selective clientele. The Marché des Enfants-Rouges, the oldest covered market in Paris, is full to bursting on Saturdays and Sundays and sells both local products and specialties from around the world.

ABOVE: The facade of the Hôtel de Ville and the square in front of it are populated by dozens of statues representing more than 100 figures from the worlds of art, science, and politics who were born in Paris. Demonstrations often fill the square. On August 25, 1944, General Charles de Gaulle gave his famous liberation of Paris speech here. The Hôtel de Ville was destroyed during the Paris Commune era but reconstructed during the Renaissance in its original form.
Opposite: Among the statues in front of the main door to the Hôtel del Ville is this lovely bronze female figure by Jules Blanchard. An allegory for *Science*, she holds a compass.
Pp. 76-77: The combination of brick and white stone in houses with slate roofs is typical of the style of the Henry IV era, seen in Place Dauphine on the Île de la Cité. This authentic royal square is one of the prettiest places in Paris. Residents have included many famous people, including Cardinal Richelieu, the Marquise de Sévigné, and Victor Hugo.

Paris

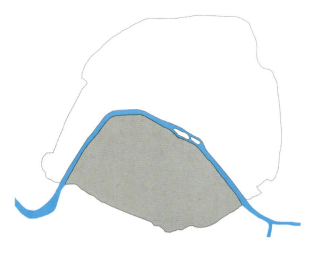

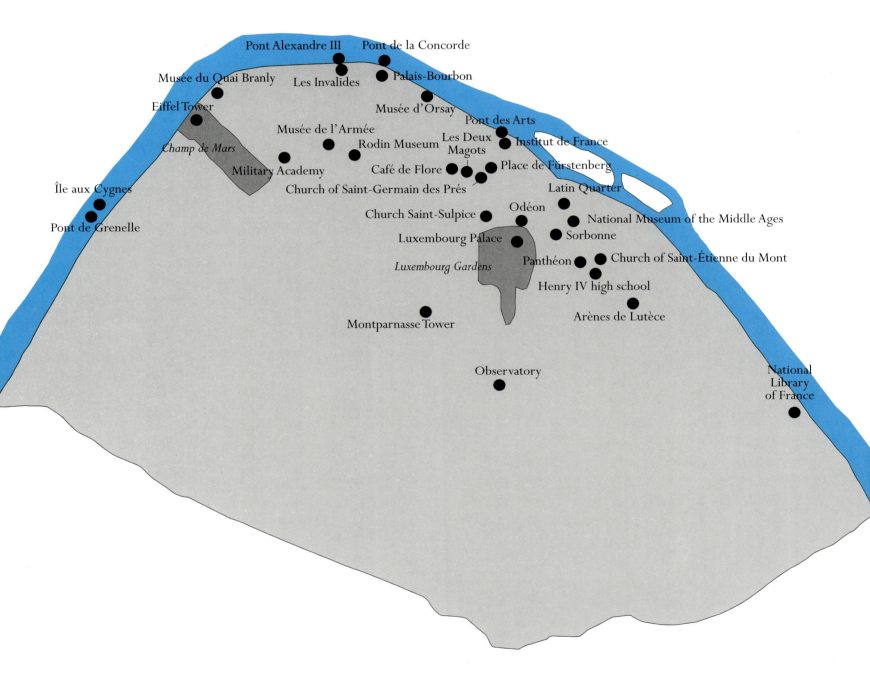

From the Latin Quarter to the Seine

Panthéon — Luxembourg — Saint-Germain-des-Prés
Palais-Bourbon — Invalides — Eiffel Tower

The Latin Quarter was the center of the city in the Roman era, along with the Île de la Cité. The Latin Quarter sits on the Left Bank of the Seine and was crossed by the main road (the cardo maximus) in Roman times; that road followed more or less the path of the Rue Saint-Jacques and Rue de la Cité, and then the Saint-Martin on the Right Bank. The ancient city of Lutetia was home to immense thermal baths, and the ruins of those can be viewed in the Musée du Cluny, the national museum of the Middle Ages at the corner of Boulevard Saint-Michel and Boulevard Saint-Germain. This museum is located largely in the enormous frigidarium covered by a vaulted ceiling fourteen and a half meters (forty-seven and a half feet) high that displays the famous Pillar of the Boatmen, which underlines the importance of the boatmen of Paris even in those early days. There is nothing left, however, of the ancient forum located at the foot of what is today Rue Soufflot. Lutetia's amphitheater, known as Les Arènes de Lutèce, has been lavishly restored and is located on Rue Monge. Today it serves as a stage for mime performances and musicals. The arena is elliptical in shape and was once the site of gladiator combat; today bocce ball and soccer are played there instead. From there, Rue Monge leads to Montagne Sainte-Geneviève, a hill that takes its name from the capital's patron saint, who in the 5th century saved the inhabitants from a Hun invasion led by Attila. At the top of this hill, the highest spot on the Left Bank, King Clovis had Geneviève buried in the church he had founded with his spouse, Clotilde. The Tower of Clovis looms—it is the only part of this building that still stands—over the walls of the prestigious Henry IV high school, one of France's top schools. During the French Revolution, the Sainte-Geneviève sanctuary was joined with the Saint-Étienne-du-Mont church, which was originally the parish of the servants of the abbey dedicated to the saint. This church is famous for its rood screen, a partition decorated in stone pierced with such fine holes that it resembles lace. Displaying clearly the influence of the Italian Renaissance, this wall separates the nave from the choral area.

The majestic Panthéon, commissioned by Louis XV, rises in the center of the square. When the king was gravely ill, he made a vow that he would build a church in honor of Saint Genevieve if he was cured. Architect Jacques-Germain Soufflot designed a huge building in the form of a Greek cross, topped with a gigantic dome. At the end of the French Revolution, the building was transformed into a secular temple to great men known as the Panthéon. It is the burial place of seventy-one famous people (including only one woman, physicist Marie Curie, whose ashes were brought here in 1995). Four more, all figures active in the Resistance, are to be added in 2015: Germaine Tillion, Geneviève de Gaulle-Anthonioz, Jean Zay, and Pierre Brossolette.

Nearby, the Sorbonne tells an ancient story that began with the building of the first seminary during the Middle Ages by a king's chaplain, Robert de Sorbon, who lent the school his name. Today a highly renowned university, the Sorbonne has maintained the 17th-century chapel, a harmonious blend of classical and Baroque style, that was commissioned by Cardinal Richelieu from the architect Jacques Lemercier. The cardinal's tomb is inside. Other buildings date to the late 19th century and include a large amphitheater that can seat 2,000 people. The Sorbonne also made history because it was the site of violent clashes during the May 1968 protests that pitted

students against the police. Right in front of the chapel on the beautiful university square with its modern fountains and trees that cast pleasant shade in the summer there are numerous cafés that beckon to passersby to stop and take a break, especially in the morning, when the area is quiet and calm. On Boulevard Saint-Michel and the surrounding lanes there are bookstores, music stores, and small movie theaters, although fast-food outlets and inexpensive clothing stores have definitely infiltrated.

The hundreds of people who stroll along the paths in the Luxembourg Gardens each day enjoy a little bit of paradise. When the weather is nice and the garden gets crowded, there can be fierce competition for the green benches in the park. The "Luco," as locals call it, offers courses in beekeeping, tai chi, chess, and tennis. The garden and the palace it serves were created by Marie de' Medici, Henry IV's widow, who wanted to get farther from the Louvre after her husband was assassinated in 1610. The queen recalled the palaces in Florence where she had spent her childhood and hired architect Salomon de Brosse to build the lovely building where France's Senate now meets. Exiting the southern end of the garden—which offers so many opportunities for walking—there are the quiet residential streets around the Paris Observatory. Created by Jean-Baptiste Colbert, a minister under Louis XIV, this scientific structure is the oldest in the world that is still in use. In this area of the capital, there is a religious congregation with a store where layettes for infants and honey made by nuns are for sale.

From the Luxembourg Gardens, the Seine can be reached via several different ancient streets, including the Rue Férou, which leads to the Church of Saint-Sulpice, an impressive building completed by architect Jean-Nicolas Servandoni in the 18th century. Inside, in the first chapel on the right, Eugène Delacroix painted one of his best known works, *Jacob Wrestling with the Angel*. In the center of the large square, a fountain incorporates statues of famous Christian orators, including Jacques-Bénigne Bossuet. Surrounding the church are plenty of charming little streets and lanes lined with adorable boutiques and popular restaurants. This area is also home to Procope, the oldest café in Paris, opened by Sicilian Francesco Procopio dei Coltelli in the late 17th century. At that time, writers and philosophers of the Age of Enlightenment drew crowds as they participated in passionate debates. Today, the Procope is still a very popular restaurant.

To the west sits one of the loveliest spots in Paris: the Place de Furstenburg, a jewel box of a square with its boutiques selling luxury items. Artist Eugène Delacroix chose well when he settled in this area, and the house where he had his studio is now open to visitors. A portion of the Abbey of Saint-Germain-des-Prés was built here. This was the first in a series of religious buildings in the area (the first church was created here in the 6th century) and an important intellectual and spiritual center in Europe for centuries. Today, the area includes two famous cafés, Café de Flore and Les Deux Magots. Once filled with writers, they are filled with tourists. While Saint-Germain may have lost a little of the bohemian flavor that it had in the days of Jean-Paul Sartre, Simone de Beauvoir, Juliette Gréco, and Boris Vian, it is still a picturesque neighborhood and one of the best places in Paris to get lost down winding narrow streets. It is a place where the past waits around every corner, as in the Cour du Commerce Saint-André or on the Rue de Buci with its colorful market next to the Odéon.

OPPOSITE: THE SAINT-ETIENNE DU MONT CHURCH IS A HAPPY MIX OF STYLES. THE BELL TOWER IS FROM THE RENAISSANCE, WHILE THE FACADE IS BOTH GOTHIC—AT THE TOP—AND BAROQUE—BELOW. IN THE 19TH CENTURY, THE BUILDING WAS RESTORED UNDER THE CARE OF VICTOR BALTARD, ARCHITECT RESPONSIBLE FOR LES HALLES. THE TOWER OF THE JUSSIEU UNIVERSITY CAN BE SEEN IN THE BACKGROUND.

From the Latin Quarter to the Seine

Opposite: *For great men, a grateful nation,* reads the inscription on the front of the Panthéon, final resting place of Victor Hugo, Jean Jaurès, Jean Moulin, and Pierre and Marie Curie. A pediment sculpture by David d'Angers depicts the fatherland crowning famous men with laurel-leaf crowns. This giant building has an arcade that references antiquity, and it stands on the Rue Soufflot, named for its architect.
Pp. 84–85: *Inside, under the dome, is Foucault's pendulum, part of an experiment the scientist conducted here in the 19th century to demonstrate the rotation of the Earth. The series of sculptures to the left is dedicated to the orators and publicists of the Restoration, including Chateaubriand, while the group on the right is consecrated "to the glory of the generals of the French Revolution." Bonaparte, astride a horse, is surrounded by his officers.*

Of course, there is no shortage of charming neighborhoods in Paris. Follow the Rue de Rennes south to Montparnasse to discover the neighborhood that during the Roaring Twenties was home to expatriate artist and writers, who flocked to the slopes of Montmartre. Between the Place du 18 Juin 1940 and the corner where the Boulevard Montparnasse crosses Rue Vavin, the boulevard is lined with the signs for famous places such as La Coupole, La Rotonde, Le Dôme, and Le Select, all of which recall those days when Ernest Hemingway, James Joyce, Sartre, Pablo Picasso, and many other artists were living in these parts.

Turning back toward the Seine from Rue Bonaparte there is the Istitut de France. Created by cardinal Jules Raymond Mazarin to cultivate gentlemen of quality, it also includes the cardinal's incredible library and is home to five different academies, including the Académie Francaise, whose serious proclamations are issued beneath the chapel's dome. In front of the institute stands the Pont des Arts, a graceful iron bridge that attracts lovers who, until just a short time ago, attached locks to the bridge as a symbol of their love. After part of the bridge's railing broke off due to the weight of the locks and fell into the river, glass panels were installed to stop people from attaching anything to the structure. West of here is the Musée d'Orsay, which sits right on the Seine. The building is an old station designed by Victor Laloux for travelers on the Paris-Orléans railway. It was opened in 1900 during the World's Fair. The metal and iron on the building's vaults are covered with a heavy stone facade. In 1939, the station—which had proven impractical—was abandoned. Forty years later, during a search for a site that would be large enough to house the impressionist collections, the management of France's museums chose the building, as it was situated conveniently in the heart of Paris. A contest was announced, with the instruction that the new design for the building would need to preserve the original station structure. The interior was then reorganized under the supervision of Milanese architect Gae Aulenti, who reconceived the spaces to be suitable for any kind of Western artwork from 1848 to 1914. The museum opened in 1986 and then was renovated once again in 2010. This time the exhibition spaces were the focus, and they were improved with an innovative lighting system. The museum houses the world's premier collection of impressionist works, from the *Dancers* of Edgar Degas to Paul Gauguin's *Tahitian Women on the Beach* to Claude Monet's *The Saint-Lazare Station*. Art Nouveau is equally well-represented with work by Victor Horta and Hector Guimard. Outside, the banks of the Seine have been given over to pedestrians since 2013. Though drivers protested, the area attracts locals and tourists alike to walk along the river in an area full of cafés, restaurants, playing fields, and park space. Directly across the river from the Madeleine Church (its counterpart from an architectural point of view), Palais Bourbon on the Right Bank owes its current facade to Napoleon. It is home to the French National Assembly, whose debates are open to the public. The pediment, created by Jean-Pierre Cortot, depicts France in a toga standing in front of her throne and accompanied by Force and Justice to call parliamentarians to the legislature. The elegant adjacent Hôtel de Lassay dates to the 1700s and is home to the president of the French National Assembly.

The Rodin Museum, located on an out-of-the-way street,

Pp. 86-87: The southern face of the Luxembourg Palace, where the Senate has met since 1958, looks out over gardens. On the edge of the large reflecting pool in the foreground, children often play with boats under the watchful eyes of their parents. The twenty-three hectares (fifty-seven acres) of French-style terraces, English gardens, and dozens of statues combine to create a peaceful setting the Parisians adore.
Opposite: In the 19th century, the Luxembourg Palace, significantly enlarged, was embellished with a new facade on the garden side. The pediment is decorated with bas-reliefs of graceful female figures by sculptor James Pradier.
Pp. 90-91: When the Luxembourg Palace was built by order of Queen Marie de' Medici, she dictated that a fountain be created in the garden that would echo the Boboli Garden of Florence and remind her of her childhood. The sculptures play out a scene from ancient mythology: the Cyclops Polyphemus has surprised Galatea, the object of his affection, in a grotto with Acis, a young shepherd, and prepares to kill them.

Paris

Opposite: The old Orsay station bears the names of the cities in western France served by the Paris-Orléans railroad. The building is a gigantic structure in steel and iron clad in stone.

Opposite: A station always needs a clock—this one is as attractive as it is useful. The initials PO, for Paris-Orléans, can be seen everywhere.

Above: The modern plan for the main entrance to the Musée d'Orsay was the work of Gae Aulenti. Its monumental limestone volumes trace the old railway tracks. The impressive steel and iron structure with its floral motifs has been preserved.

Pp. 96–97: The arcade of the Palais Bourbon is the twin to that of the Madeleine on Rue Royale on the Right Bank. The Pont de la Concorde was completed during the French Revolution and was constructed in part with stones from the Bastille. Previously the Seine could only be crossed by boat.

Pp. 98–99: The 7th Arrondissement of Paris is full of private residences. The elegant Hôtel Biron, which dates to the 1700s, was transformed into a space dedicated to art in 1908. Sculptor Auguste Rodin lived here and left his work in exchange for the hospitality. The Rodin Museum has exhibited his work since 1919.

Paris

Opposite: The dome of Les Invalides, completed in 1706, is a masterpiece of French architecture. Originally the chapel inside was exclusively for the Sun King. The surrounding gardens are perfect for a relaxing stroll.
Pp. 102-103: The paved courtyard of the Hôtel des Invalides is the site of official military ceremonies. In 1895, Captain Dreyfus was unjustly discharged here. Architect Libéral Bruant was inspired by the Escorial palace near Madrid to design the pure lines. Visitors come face-to-face with dozens of cannons upon entering. The skylights are decorated with knights' trophies and helmets.

Paris

Pp. 104–105: The Pont Alexandre III consists of a single arching span and leads to Les Invalides on the Right Bank. Houseboats on the Seine add to the local charm. The Eiffel Tower is visible in the background.
Opposite: Léopold Morice created sculptures that can be found all over Paris. This delicate *Girl with Shell* graces the Pont Alexandre III; it has been located here since 1900.
Pp. 108–109: In the late 19th century, France and Russia formed a stable alliance. These nymphs represent the Neva River and gather around the Russian coat of arms. The first brick was laid for the Pont Alexandre III, dedicated to the father of Czar Nicholas II, in 1896. The bridge opened in time for the 1900 World's Fair.

Opposite: The Eiffel Tower offers an unmistakable profile. Every evening it is lit up and it sparkles for five minutes on the hour as its beacon lights up the Paris night sky.

Pp. 112-113: The incredible metal skeleton and many beams of the Eiffel Tower are visible from all vantage points. It took workers suspended in mid-air two years (from 1887 to 1889) to join all the elements using 2.5 million rivets.

Pp. 114-115: Opened in 1973, the Montparnasse Tower is fifty-six stories high and offers a 360-degree view from the top. At 210 meters (689 feet), it is 100 meters (328 feet) shorter than the Eiffel Tower, and its foundation is 70 meters (230 feet) below ground. The Military Academy founded by Louis XV stands under the arch of the Eiffel Tower. It is located at one end of the Champs de Mars, a large green space that is a symbol of the 7th Arrondissement, consider the greenest in all of Paris.

Pp. 116-117: A fantastic view of Paris can be seen from the top of the Eiffel Tower. Just below is the Champs de Mars with its welcoming green lawn. To the left is the gilded dome of Les Invalides, next to the Panthéon, which looks tiny. In the center, behind the Military Academy, is the Montparnasse Tower.

Pp. 118-119: The Front de Seine, a neighborhood on the Seine conceived in the 1970s, consists of enormous towers built on a cement esplanade. Below the Pont de Grenelle, on the Île aux Cygnes, with its lovely walkway, the bronze copy of the Statue of Liberty in miniature is the work of Auguste Bartholdi, a native of the Alsatian city of Colmar. The sculpture was given to the city of Paris as a gift from the United States and located here for the 1889 World's Fair.

is home to a collection of the artist's works and some by his muse, Camille Claudel. The Hôtel Biron, which dates to the 18th century, was about to be demolished and was saved when the sculptor decided to rent the rooms on the ground floor to exhibit his statues. *The Age of Bronze* and *The Kiss* are among the most interesting works in this collection, along with *The Gates of Hell* and *The Burghers of Calais*. The museum's lovely garden is the perfect spot to rest and recharge under the linden trees. The Hôtel Matignon, the official residence of France's prime minister, is located on the same street. This part of Paris contains numerous other large private buildings constructed in the 18th century, when the aristocracy favored the area.

The excellent dome of Les Invalides, one of the great feats of French architecture, credited to Jules-Hardouin Mansart and more than 100 meters (328 feet) high reaches for the sky. It is covered in 550,000 sheets of gold leaf, symbolizing the power of the Sun King. Indeed, it was Louis XIV who commissioned this enormous complex shortly after undertaking the building of Versailles. Once ground was broken for the project in 1671, it was completed with incredible speed for the time. It was built to house soldiers who were injured or were on leave for other reasons, as previously they had been forced to beg to survive. Today, it is a famous hospital and retirement home. The complex also incorporates two religious buildings: the Saint-Louis-des-Invalides Chapel, also called the Soldiers' Church, and the dome where Napoleon's tomb is located. The Musée de l'Armée, which is dedicated to military art, techniques, and history, is one of the best in the world of its kind.

Still further westward, the Seine again offers a pedestrian area, and the gazes of those strolling here cannot help but be drawn to an enormous green wall covered in plants by botanist Patrick Blanc. This is the facade of the Musée du Quai Branly, commissioned by President Jacques Chirac in 1995 and designed by architect Jean Nouvel. Since opening in 2006, this new cultural landmark has earned the approval of both locals and tourists. Its rich collections take visitors on an incredible voyage through the primitive art of Africa, Asia, Oceania, and America. Its magnificent garden, the perfect place to take a break, was designed by landscape architect Gilles Clément.

From here, the outline of the Eiffel Tower can be glimpsed in the distance. Built for the World's Fair of 1889, the "iron lady" was criticized by numerous detractors and was intended to be dismantled once the exhibition ended. But at the urging of its creator, Gustave Eiffel, it was transformed into a kind of laboratory; some of the earliest telephone and radio signals, for example, were emitted from the tip of the tower. The tower would go on to become a symbol of the avant-garde and of Paris for the entire world. It was widely criticized at the time, though. The poet Paul Verlaine reported that he took a roundabout route in order not to see it and considered it a "belfry skeleton," while Guy de Maupassant derided it as "a tall skinny pyramid of iron ladders." The tower was an ambitious project on a technical level (constructed out of 18,000 pieces of metal) and it took a team working day and night and seven days a week two years and two months to complete it. Visitors who wish to visit the top—at 300 meters or 982 feet—can walk up 1,652 stairs. On the second floor, a restaurant not only serves French cuisine, but makes diners feel that they are literally suspended between heaven and earth.

Paris

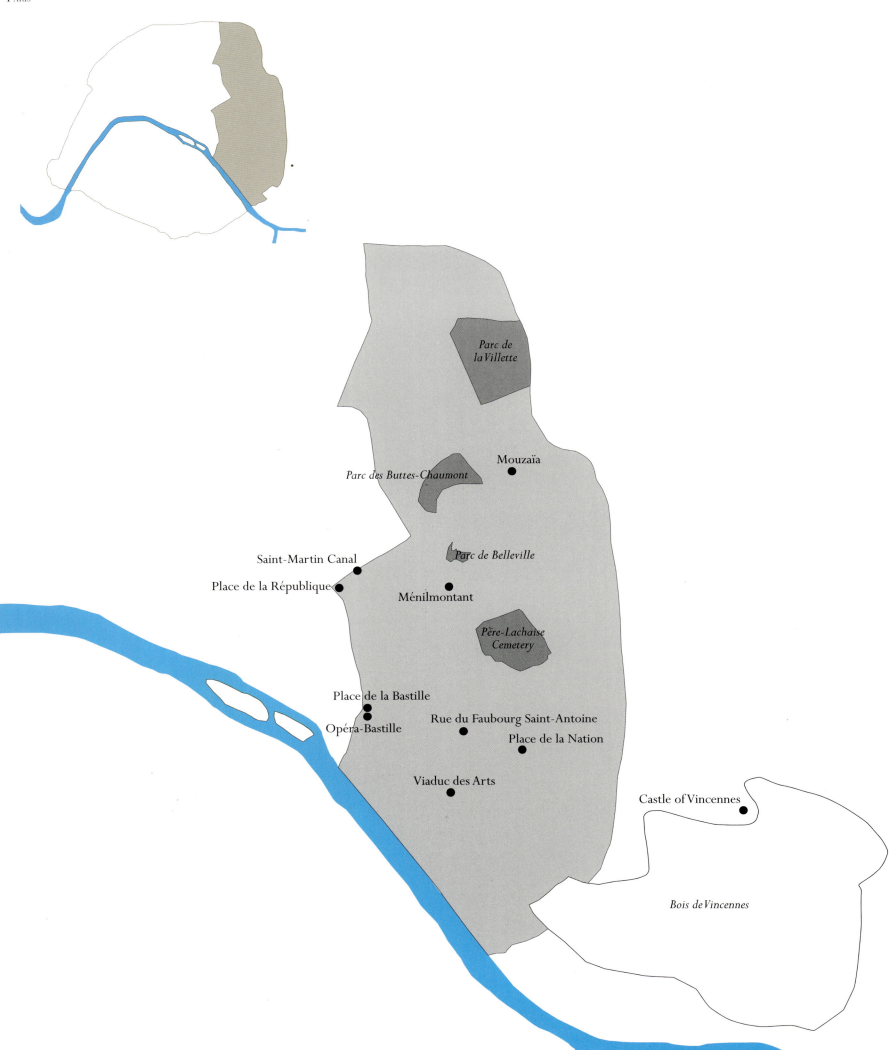

From Opéra-Bastille to the Villette

Popincourt — Reuilly — Ménilmontant — Belleville République — Buttes-Chaumont

The very mention of the Bastille brings to mind the concepts of liberty, equality, and fraternity. The Bastille, of course, is the famous prison that was stormed in 1789, but it also played a key role in the revolutions of 1830 and 1848 that roiled this working-class neighborhood in the eastern part of Paris. In the center of the Place de la Bastille stands the July Column, which commemorates those revolutions. In the Middle Ages, that spot was occupied by the Porte Saint-Antoine, which was designed to protect the east side of the capital. The kings of France passed through the area to reach the castle in Vincennes, and Charles V understood how strategically key the square could be and that there was a risk that it could be taken in a foreign invasion of the city, so he transformed the Porte Saint-Antoine into the Bastille fortress. That in turn became a state prison under Cardinal Richelieu and both Voltaire and the Marquis de Sade were imprisoned there. On July 14, 1789, this symbol of royal power fell into the hands of revolutionaries, who demolished and destroyed it completely. A few vestiges remain in the Henri-Galli square at the end of the Pont de Sully. A few decades later the Bastille neighborhood once again became inflamed: in 1830 against Charles X, and then in 1848 against Louis Philippe. Workers and craftspeople took up arms and thousands were killed by the royal troops; in 1871, they joined the Paris Commune en masse.

For centuries, the neighborhood remained a populist place. Since the end of the Middle Ages, furniture makers had established workshops in courtyards along the Rue du Fauboug Saint-Antoine. Today it's still fun to wander in and out of these when the heavy doors to the courtyards are open. Beginning in the 1980s, however, fashionable places moved to this eastern area of the capital. Old butcher shops and bread bakeries and cafés with their 1950s-style tiled floors were turned into artists' studios, start-ups, galleries, architecture firms, and more, and the original face of the Bastille got a makeover. Young people flocked to the area, and as a result trendy bars and restaurants opened. The 1989 opening of the Bastille Opera House (consider more accessible than the Palais Garnier opera, which puts on more high-end shows for the elite), designed by Canadian-Uruguayan architect Carlos Ott, sped up this radical change. The nearby Rue de Lappe still has some 1930s ballrooms, most notably the Balajo Club, the current heir to the legacy of Bastoche, an age-old cabaret. This dance club has adjusted to contemporary taste, as has the nearby club La Chapelle des Lombards, where tropical rhythms are now as common as more traditional music.

Behind the Bastille Opera House, the tree-lined street atop the Viaduc des Arts leads directly to the Bois de Vincennes, only four and a half kilometers away. In the 1990s, this old railway that at one time connected the Bastille to the villages on the banks of the Marne was turned into a park. From atop the aqueduct some beautiful architectural details not visible from street level can be enjoyed. The park is planted with hazelnut trees, linden trees, rosebushes, lavender, and other aromatic plants. The Viaduc des Arts itself runs along the Avenue Daumesnil. Glass walls were installed to turn the space under the arches into artists' studios visible to the outside. The nearby Place d'Aligre has a large market and is a popular spot where young families like to congregate, especially on Sundays.

From the large circular Place de la Nation, where many fell victim to the guillotine in an earlier era, the city turns

PP. 122-123: ALONG WITH THE PYRAMID AT THE LOUVRE, THE OPÉRA-BASTILLE IS ONE OF THE GREAT WORKS OF ARCHITECTURE CREATED DURING THE TERM OF FRANÇOIS MITTERAND. DESIGNED BY CANADIAN-URUGUAYAN CARLOS OTT, IT WAS INAUGURATED IN 1989. IT'S FAMOUS FOR ITS EXCELLENT ACOUSTICS AND FOR A SYSTEM OF PLATFORMS THAT ALLOW SCENERY TO BE CHANGED AND UNUSED SETS TO BE STORED UNDERGROUND.

north toward Ménilmontant. Like parts of Montmartre and Belleville, this area, nicknamed Ménilmuche, only became part of Paris proper in 1860. Though since the 1970s large-scale work has been underway to improve the residences here, some of the streets are still lined with small houses that make the area look like the village it once was. Maurice Chevalier was born in Ménilmontant in 1888, and the area has managed to maintain a balance of working-class life and sophistication. It was originally a hamlet of Belleville, Daniel Pennac's "Babelville," which was once crowded with taverns and dive bars where the criminals of the Belle Époque—known locally as "Apaches"—had free rein. A century later this was an immigrant community and took on a multicultural air. Rue de Belleville, lined with restaurants and stores, rises toward the Parc de Belleville with its magical vistas all the way to the hills of Saint-Cloud when the sky is clear. There are small restaurants on numerous terraces throughout, emphasizing the feeling that this is a world unto itself.

Confessor and advisor to Louis XIV François de la Chaise lived on the high ground of what is today the 20th Arrondissement in a house in the country that belonged to the Jesuits. In 1804, Napoleon had the land purchased and planted hundreds of trees and created in the area a cemetery to be used by the inhabitants of the eastern part of Paris. Though Parisians initially proved reluctant to purchase burial plots there, it earned a great deal more cachet in 1817, when the remains of Abelard and Heloise, the celebrated lovers of the Middle Ages, were transported there. With forty-three hectares (110 acres) in the shade of more than 4,000 trees, the enormous Père-Lachaise cemetery is a rich open-air museum of funerary sculpture. More than 2 million visitors annually walk along its tranquil rows to pay homage to Frédéric Chopin, Molière, Honoré de Balzac, humorist Pierre Desproges, and the other famous people buried there. In total, a million dead have been interred in the cemetery. From the cemetery the Avenue de la République leads to the Saint-Martin canal, beside the Place de la République, which was completely reorganized in 2013 in order to bring it up-to-date. Today it is decidedly contemporary in flavor. There are numerous seating areas and spaces set aside specifically for games and play, and visitors can dip their feet in the water of the fountain. This is a gathering spot for many local BoBos (bourgeois Bohemians) but also for tourists. At night the large car-free square shines with thousands of lights. The pedestal where the statue of the republic stands is illuminated. Together with the Place de la Bastille and the Place de la Nation, this is one of the most symbolic squares in Paris and a place where many large demonstrations have taken place in recent years.

The legendary Saint-Martin canal is only steps from the Place de la République. It was here, leaning on the railing of one of the bridges over the canal, that Arletty rattled off the most famous line from the film *Hôtel du Nord*: "Atmosphere! Atmosphere! Does this face look like atmosphere?" Only the facade of the Hôtel du Nord still stands today. In a picture-perfect scene, small boats glide over the water, crossing the sluices until they reach Villette basin. Dense trees lean their branches toward the water, creating a romantic covering for the walkway. On the banks of the canal people roller skate and bike in the summer and enjoy picnics until late afternoon. Small typically Parisian bistros fling their doors open to the banks of the canal, and the area is full of fashionable (and expensive) stores that have replaced the more everyday stores that once filled the area. Old warehouses demonstrate that in the 19th century this was a typical industrial neighborhood in Paris, though today it has become quite exclusive and its original structures have been put to different use. Napoleon had the Canal de l'Ourcq dug, the precursor to the Saint-

OPPOSITE: *THE GENIUS OF LIBERTY*, A GILDED BRONZE BY AUGUSTIN-ALEXANDRE DUMONT, STANDS ATOP THE BASTILLE COLUMN. IN ITS LEFT HAND IT HOLDS A BROKEN CHAIN, AND IN ITS RIGHT A FLAME. THE SCULPTOR ALSO CREATED THE DEPICTION OF NAPOLEON DRESSED AS JULIUS CAESAR AT THE TOP OF THE VENDÔME COLUMN.

Above: Close-up of the sculpted capital of the July Column in the Place Bastille. The fifty-meter (164-foot) monument is hollow inside and has 238 steps.
Opposite: The July Column at the center of the Place de la Bastille commemorates the victims of the revolutions of 1830 and 1848, many of whose remains are stored in the base. July 27, 28, and 29, 1830, known as the Trois Glorieuses, were three days of unrest that led to the end of the reign of Charles X and the installation of King Louis-Philippe. The names of 504 people who lost their lives are engraved on the column.

Paris

Opposite: The Place de la République has been closed to traffic since 2013. A statue of the Republic, with helmet and arms, stands atop the fountain holding an olive branch. Built during the Second Republic, it is accompanied by statues representing liberty, equality, and fraternity.
Pp. 130-131: Aerial view of the Père-Lachaise cemetery in the 20th Arrondissement, built on a wooded hill that at one time belonged to its namesake, confessor for Louis XIV. Napoleon commissioned the cemetery, which explains why 500 key figures from his empire are interred there. Many contemporary figures, including Edith Piaf, Jim Morrison, Simone Signoret, and Yves Montand, are buried there as well.

Opposite and p. 135: There are small chapels dotting this romantic cemetery, both marking and resisting the passage of time.
P. 134: The grave of Léon Philippe Beclard, French consul to Romania, who died in 1864 at the age of 42, features a sculpture by Gustave Crauk known as *La Douleur* that depicts a crying young woman with her arm around a bronze portrait of the consul.

From Opéra-Bastille to the Villette

Opposite: Located a hundred or so meters above sea level, the Parc de Belleville offers an unparalleled view of Paris. The park is also an ideal play space and is planted with grapevines. The fruit is harvested every year, but the wine made from the grapes is not for sale: the gardeners split it amongst themselves. The Eiffel Tower stands out amid the other buildings in the city.

From Opéra-Bastille to the Villette

Pp. 138-139: The Parc de la Villette contains a walkway that passes over the Canal de l'Ourcq. In the background are the Grands Moulins de Pantin, which today are office buildings. Next to the City of Science and Industry, the La Géode geodesic dome cinema, opened in 1985, takes up the top part of a building thirty-six meters (118 feet) in diameter. The screening room is one of the largest in the world at 1,000 square meters (10,764 square feet).

Opposite: What was once the sales hall of a meat market has become the City of Science and Industry, a parallelepiped with visible beams. The exterior of the building is completely transparent.

Martin canal, in order to provide fresh water to the city. At a later date, engineers came up with the concept of using the waterway for directing the flow of water and transporting goods. In 1825, the construction of the Saint-Martin canal got underway: it would serve as a connector between the Canal de l'Ourcq and the Villette basin from one side of the Seine to the other. Half of the canal runs underground, and it passes beneath the Boulevard Richard-Lenoir. Today, tourists can take boat rides on canals from the Seine to northern Paris and explore this unique perspective on the city. In 1863, Baron Georges-Eugène Haussmann decided to reorganize the area in and around the Parc des Buttes-Chaumont in northwestern Paris. The park was created on ancient quarries known as the "America quarries," because the gypsum that was extracted there was exported across the ocean. (Also in this neighborhood, the name of the Rue des Chaufourniers recalls the ovens that were used to burn the gypsum in order to make it into plaster.) Haussmann hired engineer Jean-Charles Alphand to create ex novo a place for the World's Fair of 1867. In a difficult site and working as best as possible with the numerous irregularities of the land due to stone extraction, Alphand designed a park that looks mountainous, where the paths are all either ascending or descending. A rocky island at the center of the lake is home to the small Temple de la Sybille, a replica of a temple at Tivoli, outside of Rome, that stands right where the ancient open-air quarry was located. A thirty-meter (ninety-eight-foot) waterfall fed by the waters of the Saint-Martin canal leads to a grotto. The idyllic Buttes-Chaumont spot feels thousands of miles away from the Monfaucon gallows, which during the Middle Ages were smack in the center of the area where the park stands today. The hanged swung there at the end of a rope. Also worth exploring in this area is Mouzaïa, sometimes known as the "America neighborhood," a fascinating spot dotted with workers' houses from the late 19th century that today sell at staggering prices.

Since 1986, the inhabitants of northeastern Paris have enjoyed the capital's largest landscaped park, the Parc de la Villette. Conceived by architect Bernard Tschumi in a rather desolate area, the fifty-five-hectare (136-acre) park was created in the spot where Baron Haussmann had once located the butchers and animal markets. Cut in two by the Canal de l'Ourcq, this unusual site can be enjoyed on foot or by bicycle. Music and science are a focus here: to the north is the City of Science and Industry; to the south is the City of Music with its museum. In 2015 the Philharmonic of Paris received a new venue with 2,400 seats here. Since its creation, the Parc de la Villette has been quite popular, and it continues to be expanded. In the summer, movies are shown outdoors. Viewers recline on folding chairs and wrap themselves snugly in blankets on the Triangle to enjoy this beloved free entertainment.

OPPOSITE: THE SAINTE CHAPELLE STANDS OUT AMID THE ROW OF BUILDINGS IN THE VINCENNES CASTLE COMPLEX. GROUND WAS BROKEN FOR THE CHURCH UNDER CHARLES V IN 1379 AND CONSTRUCTION WAS OVERSEEN BY THE TRINITY AND THE VIRGIN MARY. IT RESEMBLES THE CHAPEL ON THE ÎLE DE LA CITÉ. THE VINCENNES CASTLE WAS A ROYAL RESIDENCE WHOSE MEDIEVAL BELL TOWER STILL STANDS AND IS THE TALLEST IN EUROPE.

Paris

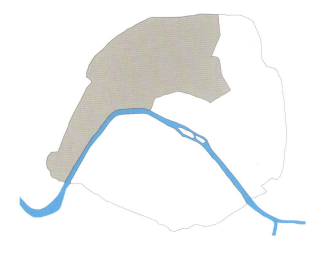

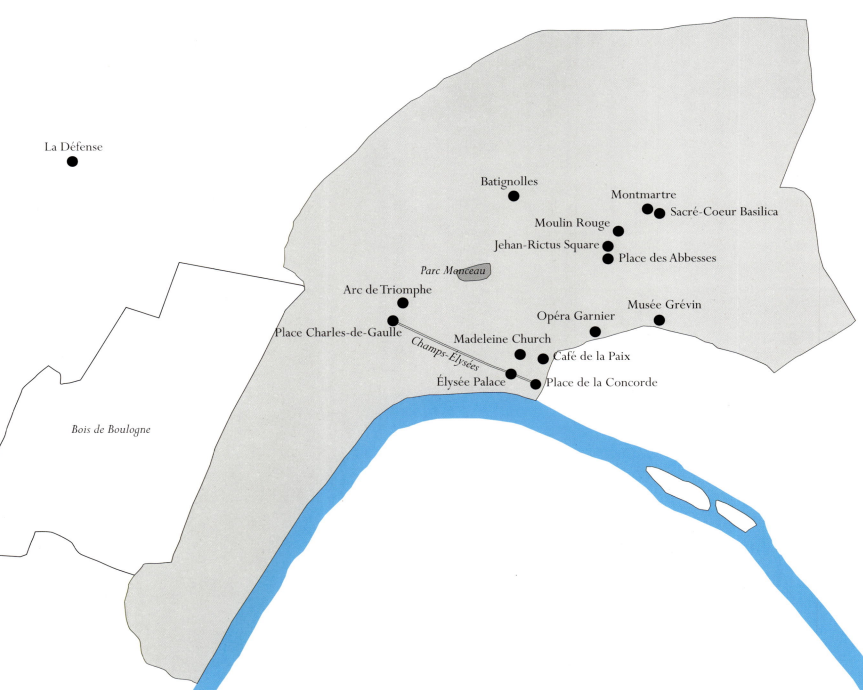

From the Champs-Élysées to Montmartre

Élysée — Opéra — Grands Boulevards — Butte Montmartre
Batignolles-Monceau — Bois de Boulogne

Flanked by the Hôtel de Crillon and the French Naval Ministry, the Place de la Concorde is hands-down the prettiest square in Paris. Designed in the form of a French garden by Jacques Ange Gabriel, the leading French architect of his day, it was known as Place Louis XV until 1792 and had a statue of the king at its heart. It was then renamed the Place de la Révolution and became the stage for numerous executions as the guillotine located there seemed to work nonstop. Louis XVI, Marie Antoinette, Georges Danton, and Maximilien Robespierre all met their fate in this square. Its current name—a nod toward peace and hope—was lent to it under the Directory. Under Louis Philippe I, eight statues representing the eight largest cities in France were installed, as were the majestic fountains that surround its most famous monument, the obelisk. This obelisk from the Temple of Amon in Luxor was donated to France by the viceroy of Egypt and unveiled in 1836 before a crowd of 300,000. It is twenty-three meters (seventy-five feet) tall and weighs 220 metric tons (242 short tons). Vehicular traffic is heavy in the area and, unfortunately, has caused significant damage to the statues.

Fewer than two kilometers away, the Champs-Élysées, the city's famous avenue, is named for the Elysian Fields of Greek mythology, the resting place for virtuous souls. This broad roadway cuts a wide swath across western Paris, linking the Place de la Concorde and its obelisk to the Place Charles de Gaulle, dominated by the Arc de Triomphe. From there, it runs all the way to the Défense district. The area between the Place de la Concorde and the Champs-Élysées rotary was laid out in 1667 by landscape architect André Le Nôtre with the intention of providing a clear and striking view of the Tuileries. At that time, this area was still largely rural, with shade trees and cows grazing in the fields. Over the centuries, and especially during the Second Empire, the avenue was refined further and altered in various ways until it took the shape we see today. Unusual luxurious buildings were built, including one owned by La Païva, a shrewd navigator of the social scene known for throwing sumptuous parties with many literati on the guest list in her neorenaissance mansion. With the Avenue Montaigne and the Avenue George V, the Champs-Élysées forms the so-called Golden Triangle, given that name due to both the presence of *haute couture* boutiques in the area and the sumptuous character of the buildings, not to mention the celebrity status of the customers and the sky-high prices of the apartments in this neighborhood. Its sidewalks are crowded day and night with tourists from around the world, hoping to bask in the glory of the stores and restaurants here, even if they can't afford their prices. This is also a site for many large-scale national celebrations. Since 1915, there has been a July 14 parade on it. In 1944, General de Gaulle marched it to mark the liberation of Paris, and in 1989 there was a massive parade organized here by Jean-Paul Goude to celebrate the bicentennial of the French Revolution. Behind the Champs-Élysées gardens stands the Elysée Palace, home to the president since 1873.

Until the late 18th century, the Place Charles de Gaulle was a wooded hillside. Today it is the hub of twelve elegant avenues that stem outward from around the Arc de Triomphe. This colossal monument, one of the city's most famous sights, was commissioned by Napoleon, who intended to have a series of triumphal arches built to memorialize his victories. Work began in 1806 and ended a mere thirty years later! In the intervening period, the motive behind the monument

PP. 146-147: THE BEAUTIFUL PLACE DE LA CONCORDE HAS THE HÔTEL DE CRILLON ON THE LEFT AND THE FRENCH NAVAL MINISTRY ON THE RIGHT, AS WELL AS TWO LARGE FOUNTAINS THAT STAND NINE METERS (TWENTY-NINE AND A HALF FEET) TALL DESIGNED BY JACQUES IGNACE HITTORFF IN THE 19TH CENTURY AND INSPIRED BY THOSE IN SAINT PETER'S SQUARE IN ROME. THE STATUES REPRESENT RIVER AND SEA NAVIGATION.

had changed: it was now determined to honor not just the Empire, but the Republic, as demonstrated by the bas-relief sculptures on its abutments. From the top of the arch, fifty meters (164 feet) in the air and accessible by elevator, there is a fantastic view all the way to the Louvre on one side and to the towers of the Défense business district on the other. On national holidays, the Tomb of the Unknown Soldier is honored here, and a torch that was introduced in 1923 is lit each evening at 6:30 p.m.

From the Place de la Concorde, the Rue Royale, with its elegant jewelry stores, leads to the neighborhood known as Madeleine, taking its name from a church. This area has variously been home to the French National Assembly, the Paris Stock Exchange, the national library, and the Temple to the Glory of the Great Army. The church is a favorite of French and international celebrities, who marry here and many of whose funerals have been held here. The imposing look of this building is lightened somewhat by the colorful flower market that surrounds it, and two well-known chefs have opened restaurants in the square.

Napoleon III commissioned construction of the Palais Garnier opera house, named for its architect, Charles Garnier. Work lasted for fourteen years, and the building was completed in 1875. The result is eclectic: within a framework of classical proportions, Garnier managed to combine many different styles. The various materials, including bronze, copper, gold leaf, mosaics, and marble, are striking in their opulence. The broad and detailed facade on the Place de l'Opéra is decorated with a large number of art-related allegorical statues, including those depicting *Dance* and *Music*. Inside, even the most jaded viewers cannot help but be impressed by the massive double staircase and four floors of arcades. In 1964, Marc Chagall lent a touch of modernity by painting the ceiling. Among the unforgettable moments that have played out in this theater are Maria Callas's unrivaled performance of Giacomo Puccini's *Tosca* in 1965.

"I love to stroll the Grands Boulevards, so many things, so many things, so many things to see," sang Yves Montand in the 1960s. Today, thousands of Parisians instead race along these Grands Boulevards. This neighborhood of offices and major banks—many of which have built beautiful Haussmannian buildings—also has a density of fast-food outlets, restaurants, stores, and movie theaters, which have replaced the chic cafés that filled the area and drew a sophisticated clientele in the 1800s. Café Tortoni, Café Frascati, Café Riche, La Maison Dorée, and their ilk—places where one might run into the poet Charles Baudelaire and his fellow dandies—have disappeared. The sole survivor is the Café de la Paix, at the corner with the Place de l'Opéra, a popular tourist destination. It has preserved its original decor (mirrors, plaster columns, and scenes from mythology painted on the ceiling) by Charles Garnier. The Grands Boulevards were built in the 17th century after the bastions that protected Paris to the north and east were destroyed. In their place, private buildings and theaters popped up one after the other. Later, after part of the neighborhood was demolished, Baron Haussmann had five-story buildings built—recognizable by their iron balconies—along "his" boulevards, and he also ordered the installation of streetlights, some of which are still in place today. Along the Grands Boulevards there are covered walkways filled with the variety of shops and museums for which Paris is famous: antique shops, museums (including the Musée Grévin wax museum), and bookstores speak to another era and beckon to passersby to come in and explore.

Located atop a hill of the same name in the north of the capital, Montmartre is one of the city's most unique neighborhoods. At one time a suburb (it became part of Paris proper in 1860), it has maintained its own special

Opposite: The long profile of the obelisk behind the fountain in the Place de la Concorde.

Pp. 150-151: Aerial view of the Right Bank from the Place de la Concorde and, beyond that, from the Rue de Rivoli, which borders the Tuileries gardens.

From the Champs-Elysées to Montmartre

Opposite: The gates of the eclectic Petit Palais are topped with the coat of arms of Paris. Built for the 1900 World's Fair, it is now the museum of fine arts of Paris. Its collections range from antiquities to items from the early 20th century. A café under one of the arcades on the internal courtyard is a recent addition.

Above: Aerial view of the Grand Palais and its incredible glass vault. The central portion of the building hosts cultural exhibitions, while the wings are home to the national galleries, temporary exhibitions, and a science museum. The Petit Palais can be seen behind it: both buildings were built for the 1900 World's Fair.
Opposite: The glass of the Grand Palais and some of its splendid metal decoration.

Above: The courtyard of the Élysée Palace, home to the president.
Opposite: A close-up of the building's facade. The Élysée Palace was built in the 13th century and was home to Madame Pompadour. The building is open to the public every year in September during the European Heritage Days and it draws record numbers.
Pp. 158-159: The top of the Arc de Triomphe provides the best view of the Champs-Elysées in all its splendor. Its wide sidewalks are crowded with tourists. Two kilometers (one and a quarter miles) in the distance sits the Place de la Concorde.

Paris

Opposite: The enormous Arc de Triomphe looms over the Champs-Élysées. On the right side of the base is François Rude's sculpture *Departure of the Volunteers of 1792*, which depicts volunteers from Marseille who introduced the song that gave rise to *La Marseillaise*. On the left is *The Triumph of 1810* by Jean-Pierre Cortot with Napoleon at the center.
Pp. 162-163: Close up of *The Triumph of 1810* by Jean-Pierre Cortot, which dates to 1833. Left of Napoleon (who commissioned the construction of the Arc de Triomphe) is a woman who represents history writing about the emperor's triumph on a tablet. Above Napoleon's head are trumpets and an imperial eagle.

Above: The Madeleine Church, whose columned facade (giving it the look of an ancient temple) is the mirror image of the front of the Palais Bourbon on the Left Bank. A wide staircase leads to the entrance. Classical music concerts are often held in the Madeleine.
Opposite: Close-up of the pediment of the Madeleine Church featuring Philippe-Henri Lemaire's *Last Judgment*.
Pp. 166-167: On the Place de l'Opéra, a Parisian crossroads along the Grands Boulevards, the Palais Garnier shines with gold and marble. The facade is a prime example of the ostentation typical of the Second Empire. On the roofs, two series of gilded bronzes by Charles Gumery represent *Poetry*, left, and *Harmony*, right.

PARIS

PP. 168-169: THE LARGE ATRIUM OF THE OPERA HOUSE WAS BASED ON THE ARCADES OF RENAISSANCE CASTLES: IMPRESSIVE SIZE, DUAL COLUMNS, SPARKLING GOLD, ELABORATE MIRRORS THAT REFLECT LIGHT EVERYWHERE, AND PAINTED SCENES FROM MYTH ON THE CEILING.
OPPOSITE: CLOSE-UP OF THE CEILING IN THE OPERA HOUSE'S ENTRY HALL WITH ALLEGORICAL PAINTINGS BY PAUL BAUDRY.

FROM THE CHAMPS-ÉLYSÉES TO MONTMARTRE

OPPOSITE: Close-up, *Dance* statue, Palais Garnier.

Opposite and above: The Galeries Lafayette, one of the city's large department stores, is topped by an intricate neo-Byzantine glass dome created by master glass craftsman Jacques Gruber. The interior of the store resembles a theater.
Pp. 176-177: Printemps on Boulevard Haussmann opened in 1865. This 1889 facade was designed by Paul Sédille in typical Second Empire style.
P. 178: Statues adorn the clock on the facade of the Gare de l'Est. The Rhine and the Seine are represented by works by Jean-Louis Brian.
P. 179: Gare du Nord. Statues depict, from left to right, Lille, Amiens, Rouen, and Arras.

From the Champs-Elysées to Montmartre

Opposite: Montmartre's Sacré-Coeur Basilica can be seen through the windows of the large clock of the Musée d'Orsay on the opposite bank of the Seine.

Opposite: Sacré-Coeur Basilica sits atop a large hill that can make for a challenging climb, but those who do reach the top are rewarded with an exceptional view. On opposite sides of the church, Joan of Arc and Saint Louis clutch their swords and strike out at their enemies.

OPPOSITE: THOUGH ONLY THE PROPELLER IS ORIGINAL, THE MOULIN ROUGE CABARET, BIRTHPLACE OF THE CAN-CAN, STILL HOSTS SHOWS THAT ARE ENTHUSIASTICALLY ATTENDED BY TOURISTS WITH A LOVE FOR MONTMARTRE.
PP. 186-187: AERIAL VIEW OF THE CHAILLOT, HOME TO TWO MUSEUMS, ONE OF THE FOUR NATIONAL THEATERS IN PARIS (WHICH HAS THREE STAGES), AND A SERIES OF GARDENS THAT SLOPE DOWN TOWARD THE SEINE. THE COMPLEX WAS BUILT ON THE PLACE DU TROCADÉRO FOR THE WORLD'S FAIR IN 1937. THE OPEN SPACE IN FRONT OF THE EIFFEL TOWER, BAPTIZED THE PARVIS DES DROITS DE L'HOMME, OR RIGHTS OF MAN ESPLANADE, IS OFTEN A SITE FOR DEMONSTRATIONS.
PP. 188-189: IN THE CHAILLOT, THE NAVAL MUSEUM ON THE LEFT AND THE CITÉ DE L'ARCHITECTURE ET DU PATRIMOINE ON THE RIGHT KEEP WATCH OVER THE TROCADÉRO FOUNTAINS THAT STAND IN THE CENTER OF THE GARDENS. THE PLAY OF WATER IS QUITE STRIKING.

character. Indeed, just the name Montmartre is closely linked to the bohemian atmosphere of the Belle Époque and its cabarets. The memory of Henri de Toulouse-Lautrec still floats around this hill, as well as that of La Goulue, a dancer at the Moulin-Rouge, and the singer Aristide Bruant, who performed every evening at the Le Chat Noir club. No other neighborhood can boast such a long list of painters who once took up residence: impressionists, Fauves, cubists. Pierre-Auguste Renoir, Vincent Van Gogh, Raoul Dufy, and Maurice Utrillo had their studios in what is now the Musée de Montmartre, while the Bateau-Lavoir provided workspace for Pablo Picasso, Kees Van Dongen, Maurice de Vlaminck, Amedeo Modigliani, and so many more. Renoir and Van Gogh were part of the regular clientele at the Au Lapin Agile, as were writers, including Guillaume Apollinaire, Francis Carco, and Max Jacob. There are still a few artists living in Montmartre today, but they reside in the comfortable houses hidden behind high walls on streets like Avenue Junot. That street was created in 1912, when the area, then known as Maquis, was still relatively uninhabited and dotted with wooden shacks. Designer Francisque Poulbot lived in Maquis then, and his drawings of the Gavroche street urchin character became so famous that the French began to refer to street kids as *petits poulbots*. Place du Tertre is filled with portrait artists on Sundays and souvenir stands sell kitschy miniatures in Montmartre, a faint echo of its rich artistic heritage.

The slopes of the Montmartre hill have become increasingly chic—and expensive. The lively Rue des Abbesses and Place des Abbesses are today lined with restaurants and fashionable stores; in the Jehan-Rictus square, *Le Mur des Je t'Aime (I Love You: The Wall)* is covered with declarations of love in 250 different languages. In 1937, grapes began to be grown on the hill again, and these days a healthy harvest yields enough fruit for about 2,000 bottles of Clos-Montmartre.

At the top of Montmartre's hill, the Sacré-Coeur Basilica was built at the behest of two Catholic businessmen who vowed to create the building in reaction to France's participation in the Franco-Prussian War of 1870. Construction began five years later under architect Paul Abadie, who was influenced by the Roman-Byzantine church of Périgueux Cathedral dedicated to Saint Front. The heart of one of the two creators, Alexandre Legentil, is kept in an urn in the crypt. The shape of the church, its dome, and its white limestone, which shines even more brilliantly after it rains, can be seen from afar and are a fixed point in the Paris skyline. Though once windmills dotted the Montmartre landscape, only one survives today—the Moulin de la Galette. It was formerly a music-hall, but today it's private property.

In the western part of the capital sits the charming Batignolles neighborhood, immortalized by Henri Fantin-Latour in *A Studio at Les Batignolles*. Squares, churches, markets, and low-rise houses give this neighborhood the look and feel of a small village, which is what Batignolles was until 1830. At the time this outlying village near the Monceau plain was home to the working class. In the 19th century, it was the focus of frenzied speculation, accurately described by Honoré de Balzac and Émile Zola in their novels. The bourgeoisie arrived and brought with them buildings on high ground next to the Parc Monceau; these days, many foreign residents are drawn to this quiet and discreet neighborhood of wide avenues. Further west is a majestic street that breaks all records: 120 meters (394 feet) wide by one and a half kilometers (almost a full mile) long, the Avenue Foch was created during the Second Empire to connect the Bois de Boulogne, which had recently been fixed up, to the city. Embassies and luxurious private residences sit behind high walls that keep prying eyes away. The street leads to the Bois de Boulogne, the city's second largest park after the Bois de Vincennes and home to the Louis Vuitton Foundation (the most recently opened museum in Paris). The impressive glass building that is home to the museum slants toward the sky with twelve glass "sails." It was designed by American-Canadian Frank Gehry, the architect behind the Guggenheim Museum Bilbao in Spain. Bernard Arnault, chairman of the LVMH Group, a luxury goods giant, inaugurated the building and the foundation in 2014.

From the Champs-Elysées to Montmartre

Pp. 190–191: This open space in the Défense district is a large car-free zone with gracefully modern skyscrapers. The area is a busy one: 170,000 people work for 3,600 different companies, and 450,000 people pass through the district each day on the RER A express railway.
P. 192: Modern architecture with geometric lines is exhibited in the buildings of the Défense district, which create all kinds of interesting reflections.
P. 193: The large canopy under the Grande Arche, a cube-shaped triumphal arch erected in 1989, is held up by wires.
Opposite: The CNIT was the first building constructed in the Défense district and went up in 1957. Its triangular reinforced concrete vault with a 218-meter (715-foot) span held up by three points of support was revolutionary at the time. Today there are a few dozen stores in the CNIT building.

Paris

The Royal Residences

Versailles — Fontainebleau — Vaux-le-Vicomte — Chantilly

Versailles

The Palace of Versailles, added to the UNESCO World Heritage List in 1979, was the fruit of the unbridled ambition of Louis XIV, the Sun King, who wanted more than anything to trumpet his power and his reign to the entire world. The palace has become a symbol of the inventiveness of the artists the king managed to recruit to carry out this project worthy of an Egyptian pharaoh. Architects Louis Le Vau and Jules Hardouin-Mansart (responsible for the Hall of Mirrors), painter and decorator Charles Le Brun, and landscape designer André Le Nôtre were summoned to work on this truly superlative residence and its grounds. It took fifty years and 30,000 workers to complete it.

The building is a maze of enormous size with 2,300 rooms where thousands of courtiers, guards, and servants could live. The superb gardens are a major part of the palace's identity—among other things Versailles was meant to serve as the king's loud and prideful response to the superintendent of finances, who he thought believed himself to be the king's equal. When Nicolas Fouquet organized a famously opulent August 17, 1661 party at his castle in Vaux-le-Vicomte, he unintentionally inspired the creation of Versailles. Louis XIV decided to build a palace that would be more over-the-top in terms of luxury and beauty than any the world had ever seen—including, perhaps especially, the one in Vaux-le-Vicomte.

In 1631, Louis XIII had started construction of a modest castle to replace a hunting lodge near a forest full of wild game. When Louis XIV got involved, the young king instead ordered terraced gardens decorated with flowerbeds and topiary, as well as abundant sculptures and fountains. Beginning in 1668, bolstered by his military successes, he decided to have built around the ancient castle enormous Italian-style buildings with flat roofs and long white-stone facades made elaborate with columns and pillars. As time went on, more buildings were added, because the king wanted to live at Versailles and make it the seat of his government. In 1710, the splendid chapel designed by Robert de Cotte was completed. Versailles included a marble structure known as the Grand Trianon. Louis XV, the Sun King's successor, had some private apartments built inside the enormous palace and hired architect Jacques Ange Gabriel to build the charming Petit Trianon and the Opéra. At a later date, Louis XVI commissioned the queen's wing for Marie Antoinette.

With 7.5 million visitors annually, the Palace of Versailles is one of France's most visited sites. The Hall of Mirrors is its most famous room. Sixty-five meters (213 feet) long and ten meters (33 feet) wide, it is lit by the light that shines through seventeen windows and then reflects off mirrored panels. The ceiling was painted by Charles Le Brun during the first seventeen glorious years of the reign of Louis XIV from 1661 to 1678. The designer truly thought of everything: the sun rises at just the right place for the windows and the mirrors, and there is a view of the grand canal and the sun setting beneath the horizon beyond it, all a highly symbolic homage to the greatness of the Sun King.

Fontainebleau

The Palace of Fontainebleau is definitely one of the royal residences that has seen the comings and goings of the largest number of crowned heads. The palace

Pp. 198-199: Versailles was the spectacular residence of the French monarchy from Louis XIV to Louis XVI and a model of magnificence for the courts throughout Europe. The castle's French gardens, designed by André Le Nôtre, decorated with fountains, are a highlight. Here, two rectangular pools reflect light and illuminate the building and the Hall of Mirrors. Le Nôtre used both light and plants as decorative elements.

THE ROYAL RESIDENCES

OPPOSITE: ON THE TERRACE, WHERE TWO LARGE POOLS OF WATER REFLECT THE BUILDING'S FACADE, FOUR STATUES DECORATE THE MARBLE BORDERS OF THE POOLS. THESE WORKS ARE THE PERSONIFICATIONS OF RIVERS: THE SEINE, BY ÉTIENNE LE HONGRE, RECLINES BY THE NORTH POOL.

PP. 202-203: THE MARBLE COURTYARD WAS THE FIRST SECTION OF THE CASTLE TO BE BUILT AND WAS A HUNTING LODGE DESIGNED BY PHILIBERT LE ROY IN 1631 AND FINISHED BY LOUIS LE VAU AND JULES HARDOUIN-MANSART, WHO ADDED THE BALUSTRADES AND THE STATUES. THE MARBLE COURTYARD—MADE OF STONE AND BRICK—DID DOUBLE DUTY AS A STAGE FOR SOME OF MOLIÈRE'S PLAYS. THE CENTRAL BALCONY IS OFF THE BEDROOM OF LOUIS XIV.

THE ROYAL RESIDENCES

OPPOSITE: IN THE PARTERRE OF THE GRANDE ORANGERIE OF VERSAILLES, PLANTS DRAW ARABESQUES AROUND A CENTRAL REFLECTING POOL. THE SUN KING HAD 1,000 CRATES OF LEMON TREES, OLEANDERS, PALM TREES, AND ORANGE TREES BROUGHT HERE FROM SPAIN, PORTUGAL, AND ITALY.

PP. 206-207: THE JACQUES ANGE GABRIEL-DESIGNED FLOWERBEDS IN FRONT OF THE CROSS-SHAPED FRENCH PAVILION IN THE GARDENS OF THE PETIT TRIANON ARE BASED ON AN ENVIRONMENTALLY SOUND SYSTEM: EACH PLANT IS BURIED IN ITS OWN CONTAINER, WHICH HELPS CONSERVE WATER AND MAKES FREQUENT CHANGES POSSIBLE.

PP. 208-209: THE HALL OF MIRRORS WITH ALMOST 200 MIRRORS WAS PART OF THE GRANDS APPARTEMENTS. THIS GRAND GALERIE, AS IT WAS CALLED IN THE 17TH CENTURY, WAS USED DAILY AS A PASSAGEWAY AND ALSO A PLACE FOR MEETINGS AND INTRODUCTIONS FOR MEMBERS OF THE COURT AND VISITORS.

was inhabited continuously by kings and emperors of France for seven centuries and an astonishing thirty-four monarchs were seated there. Napoleon called it "the house of ages," a concise description of the starring role it played in the history of France's dynasties, from the Capetians to the Orléans, the Valois, the Bourbons, and the Bonapartes. With more than 1,500 rooms arranged in the heart of 130 hectares (321 acres) of gardens, the Palace of Fontainebleau is a crucial part of the history of France.

The Palace of Fontainebleau was originally a small fortified castle built in the 12th century. It was Francis I who, seduced by a nearby immense forest perfect for hunting (one of his favorite pastimes) expanded it to its current size. Additionally, after his imprisonment in Spain (under the thumb of Charles V), the king understood that he should be close to Paris, so he left behind his castles in the Loire Valley. Over a decade he completely remodeled the ancient Medieval fortress (only one rampart remains) according to the Italian Renaissance canon. From Italy he summoned well-known fresco painters and stucco artists who worked under Rosso Fiorentino and the Bolognese Francesco Primaticcio. The decor created by these artists was the foundation of the so-called Fontainebleau school. In the massive Gallery of Francis I, sixty meters (197 feet) long by six meters (twenty feet) wide, work by this artist illustrates royal power: the F with a crown and the salamander, emblems of Francis I, are visible all over and the scenes from mythology are clearly intended as references to the sovereign's glory. Below that, in the baths, the king amassed an extraordinary collection of Italian paintings; his second-floor library included incredible manuscripts from Italy and the East. The Gallery of Ulysses, 150 meters (492 feet) long, has walls and a vaulted ceiling covered completely with paintings modeled on Raphael's Vatican loggia with scenes from *The Odyssey*. The ballroom, one of the highlights, decorated by Nicolò dell'Abate based on a design by Primaticcio, was completed under Henry II, whose crest adorns the spectacular coffered walnut ceiling.

The succeeding kings made numerous changes (Henry IV expanded the castle, and then Louis XIV, Louis XV, and Louis XVI made their own changes), especially in the decor for the apartments. After the French Revolution, Napoleon, who preferred Fontainebleau over Versailles, made the bedroom of the king into the throne room. Numerous other rooms in the palace bear his mark, and a wing is given over to a museum that bears his name. In the Cheval Blanc courtyard, the site of tournaments during the reign of Francis I, Napoleon bid adieu to his Old Guard on April 20, 1814.

Vaux-le-Vicomte

In a rural area northeast of Melun (today located in Seine-et-Marne), Nicolas Fouquet, superintendent of finances under Louis XIV, in 1656 invited three young artists from the Grand Siècle, architect Louis Le Vau, painter Charles Le Brun, and landscape architect André Le Nôtre, to create a home fit for a king. Fouquet had shot to success and was one of the richest men in France in his day. Drunk on his own power, he chose as his motto *Quo non ascendet?* (What heights will he not scale?) Work on the Vaux-le-Vicomte castle lasted five years and involved 18,000 workers.

Fouquet invited Louis XIV to the opening of his palace on August 17, 1661. The king came with his mother, Anne of Austria, his brother Philippe, and members of his court. They received an incredible welcome. The superintendent had asked his chef, François Vatel, to create a twenty-four-

Opposite: One of the rooms in the Appartements de Mesdames boasts especially refined decoration. The Mesdames de France were the daughters of Louis XV, who moved to the castle in 1752. Only two of them, Adelaide and Victoire (who never married and lived to an old age), resided in the apartments until the time of the French Revolution.

THE ROYAL RESIDENCES

Opposite: Close-up of the stuccos in the Salon of Apollo. Louis XIV identified with the god of sun, arts, and peace, and the room was at one time the most opulent in Versailles, as can still be seen in the ceiling decoration. The sculptures are all circular and completely covered in gold. From 1673 to 1682 this was the king's bedroom, and it then became the throne room, where the king granted audiences.

Pp. 214-215: The War Room, along with the Peace Room, frames the Hall of Mirrors. The stucco relief by Antoine Coysevox depicts *Louis XIV Victorious Crowned by Glory*. Trophies adorn the walls.

THE ROYAL RESIDENCES

Pp. 216–217: The staircase in the famous Cheval Blanc courtyard at Fontainebleau was designed by Jean Androuet du Cerceau in the 17th century. Large royal processions passed through this courtyard, and it was here that Napoleon bid adieu to his Old Guard before leaving for Elba.
Opposite: Italian Renaissance artists decorated the Gallery of Francis I. The elephant was a symbol of wisdom and regal character. The F for Francis I and his emblem, the salamander, are visible on the panels.
Pp. 220–221: In the Gallery of Francis I, a fresco depicting *The Nymph of Fontainebleau* was created by Louis-Charles-Auguste Couder in 1834 based on an engraving by Pierre Milan in the 1500s. The letter F, for Francis I, was incorporated into the decor, as was the salamander, his personal emblem.

219

PARIS

OPPOSITE: STUCCO IN THE GALLERY OF FRANCIS I AT FONTAINEBLEAU.
PP. 224–225: THE IMPOSING FACADE OF THE VAUX-LE-VICOMTE CASTLE, WHICH WAS BUILT ON A TERRACE SURROUNDED BY A MOAT. THE CLERESTORY WINDOWS IN THE DOME OFFER A MAGNIFICENT VIEW OF THE ENTIRE PARK.

course dinner with thirty forms of refreshment and five specialties based on pheasant, quail, ortolan, partridge and other game birds served from gold-plated platters and eaten off of silver dishes. A violin orchestra played compositions by Jean-Baptiste Lully, superintendent for music; afterward, in the park, the Molière play *Les Fâcheux*, a comedy-dance created specially for the occasion, was performed. Fireworks in the shape of a fleur-de-lis, the royal emblem, lit the gardens and rockets were launched from the top of the dome to create an arc of light, a representation of the glory of the Sun King and of Fouquet himself. But Fouquet would pay dearly for his proud display. Nineteen days later, Louis XIV had him arrested by d'Artagnan. Fouquet's possessions were confiscated, and after a three-year-long trial, the king ordered the superintendent to be condemned to prison for the rest of his life.

Today Vaux-le-Vicomte is the largest private estate in France. This exceptional complex has survived remarkably well over time and accounts for 500 hectares (1,236 acres), one and a half hectares (three and three quarter acres) of which are occupied by buildings, forty-five hectares (111 acres) by gardens, and thirteen kilometers (eight miles) of avenues. The interiors are a profusion of frescoes, gilded details, and stuccos. In the gardens, Le Nôtre created a series of optical illusions that make visitors feel that the entire gigantic park can be taken in at one glance. Even before his outstanding work at Versailles, the landscape architect played with placing water in a starring role here: the facades of the castle are reflected in all the surrounding bodies of water, and there are terraces and fountains that descend down toward the Grand Canal.

Chantilly

Property of the Institut de France, the Château de Chantilly was a royal residence. Over the centuries many castles and fortresses were built on the site of an ancient Gallo-Roman city before the property came into the hands of Anne de Montmorency (a man, despite the name), who was a member of one of France's oldest families. This very rich man was said to own 130 castles! He'd grown up with François d'Angoulême, the future Francis I, and he served five kings and joined the royal family by marrying a cousin of Francis I. In 1560, he called upon the most prestigious artists of the day, including Bernard Palissy, Léonard Limosin, and Jean Goujon, to decorate his Petit Château.

In the 17th century, Henri de Bourbon-Condé and his wife, Charlotte Catherine de la Trémoille, inherited Chantilly and then left it to his son, the Grand Condé (a cousin of Louis XIV), who decided to embellish the existing castle and called on Le Nôtre to create water features that were so elaborate that the Sun King did everything in his power to overshadow them when he commissioned the gardens for Versailles.

In 1830, the latest Prince de Condé, owner of the château but without heirs after the death of his son, the Duke of Enghien, left all his property to his nephew, Henri d'Orléans, Duke of Aumale. He had the Grand Château, which had not survived the French Revolution, rebuilt in Renaissance style. A lover of painting, he also amassed an incredible collection that included Raphael's *Three Graces*, Jean Antoine Watteau's *Le Donneur de Sérénades*, Jean-Auguste-Dominique Ingres's *Self-Portrait*, and a series of famous portraits by François Clouet. Among the 13,000 volumes in his library was the manuscript for *Très Riches Heures du Duc de Berry*, and he also exhibited a collection of extraordinary gems and precious stones, including the pink diamond known as the Gran Condé. These and other treasures were bequeathed to the Institut de France in 1897.

OPPOSITE: THE KING'S ROOM AT VAUX-LE-VICOMTE. ELSEWHERE, IN HOMAGE TO LOUIS XIV, A CROWN TOPS WINDOWS THAT OVERLOOK AN OVAL REFLECTING POOL.

THE ROYAL RESIDENCES

Opposite: Stuccos with gold leaf decorate the king's room at Vaux-le-Vicomte, which was recently restored. **Pp. 230-231:** Fouquet was enamored with the figure of Hercules, a symbol of power, and the antechamber to his apartments is dedicated to the strongman. *The Apotheosis of Hercules* clearly alludes to the superintendent's power and success.

Opposite: The Château de Chantilly, reconstructed in the 19th century in the Renaissance style, and its elegant garden with its many water features.
Pp. 234–235: The Petit Chateau of Chantilly, left, and the Grand Chateau, right.
Pp. 236–237: Ornamental shrubbery in the gardens at Chantilly.

The Royal Residences

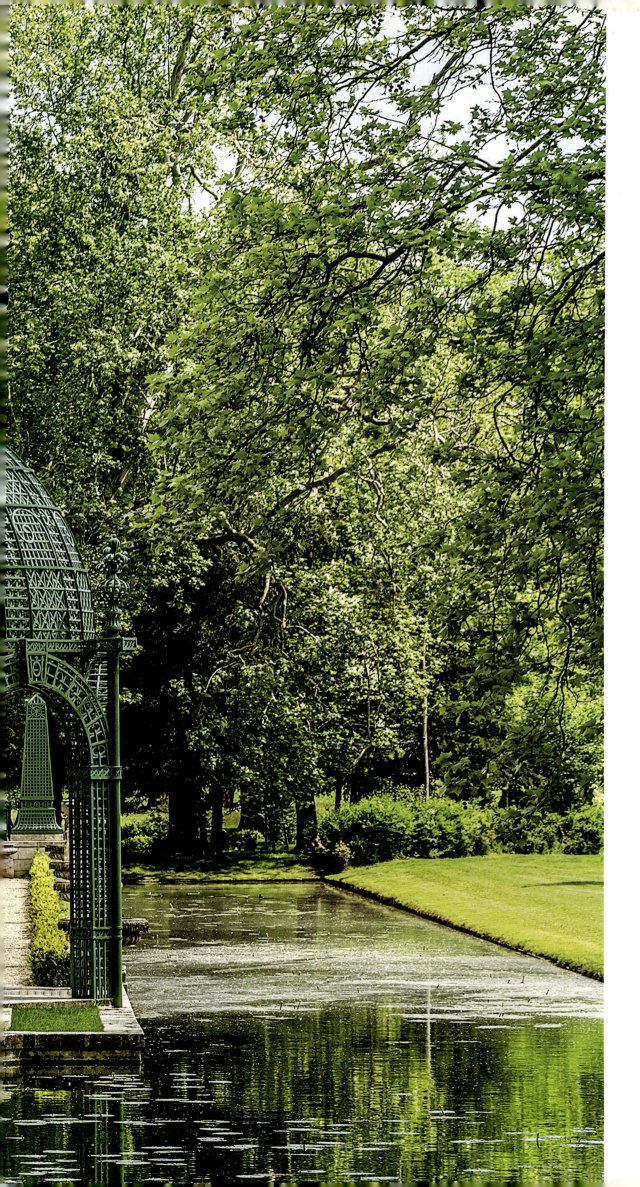

Opposite: The Island of Love is just one of the buildings that dot the English-style gardens at Chantilly.

PHOTOGRAPHIC CREDITS

All photographs are from the ©Shutterstock online archive, in particular:

pp. 16-17, 165: ©Zvonimir Atletic
pp. 28-29: ©Kanuman
pp. 32-33, 94: ©Dmitry Brizhatyuk
pp. 36-37: ©Doin Oakenhelm
pp. 38-39: ©Christian Bertrand
pp. 40-41, 44-45, 176-177, 193: ©Kiev.Victor
pp. 70-71: ©Charles Leonard
p. 74: ©Nightman1965
pp. 84-85: ©posztos
p. 95: ©Bargotiphotography
pp. 118-119: ©lapas77
p. 134: ©Martchan
pp. 146-147: ©Penka Todorova Vitkova
pp. 168-169: ©Frederic Legrand
p. 184: ©lornet
pp. 190-191: ©Nikonaft
p. 192: ©Christian Mueller
pp. 194-195: ©Radu Razvan

Other credits:
pp. 208-209, 212-213, 214-215, 218-219, 220-221, 222-223, 226, 228-229, 230-231: ©Luca Sassi – Sassi Editore Srl

SASSI171221CV/ Printed in March 2018 in China.